CRYSTAL POWER

PATENT NO. 4,448,443

CRYSTAL POWER
THE ULTIMATE PLACEBO EFFECT

Lawrence E. Jerome

PROMETHEUS BOOKS
Buffalo, New York

Library of Congress Card Catalog No. 89-60082
ISBN 0-87975-532-6

Dedicated to
Isadora Fisher,
who began reading at the age of 6 months,
was writing at the age of 12 months,
and is published at the age of 18 months.

TABLE OF CONTENTS

ACKNOWLEDGMENTS

Hundreds of people have contributed to my research and understanding of crystal power; each in his own way has contributed to this book, and to each I offer my sincere thanks.

I especially wish to thank Professor Paul Kurtz, editor-in-chief of Prometheus Books, for his support and encouragement of this project.

Kent Harker, editor of *BASIS,* deserves the initial credit in steering me toward the study of crystal power.

Don Oldenburg of *The Washington Post* likewise deserves credit for first suggesting, "Isn't this 'crystal power' something like a placebo effect?"

I am indebted to Dael Walker, owner of the Crystal Shop in Pacheco, California, for taking the time to explain his crystal power experiments, which I have replicated and described in this book.

I am also greatly indebted to Jerome Clark, editor of *Fate,* and Merle Berk, editor of *Lapidary Journal,* both of whom supported my Crystal-Power Survey by letting me use their publications as a vehicle to reach crystal workers.

To all the others who contributed, again my sincere thanks.

Lawrence Jerome
San Jose, California

1

CRYSTAL POWER: THE SEARCH BEGINS

On December 7, 1987, crystal power made the front cover of *Time* magazine: a grinning Shirley MacLaine was pictured holding a handful of quartz and amethyst crystals, with the caption, "Om . . . THE NEW AGE, Starring Shirley MacLaine, faith healers, channelers, space travelers and crystals galore."

Now there could be no doubt: crystal power had arrived! If crystals could make the front cover of *Time,* surely they *must* have some power—perhaps not as much as Mikhail Gorbachev, *Time's* "Man of the Year" in 1987—but certainly power enough to capture the imagination and attention of the richest, most powerful nation on earth. The *Time* article didn't just focus on crystals but treated in typical tongue-in-cheek reportorial style the full range of New Age beliefs and activities: astrology, reincarnation, the Harmonic Convergence attended by thousands atop various mountains across the nation, as well as herbs, homeopathy, spirit communication, and a host of other esoteric beliefs that seem totally out of sync with today's scientific, materialistic world.[1]

Regardless of what one might think of the New Age and all its odd beliefs, the *Time* article—and especially the front cover—made one fact crystal clear: crystals and their alleged "power" are an integral driving force behind the current surge of interest in esoteric spiritualism, especially in faith healing, spirit communication (channeling), and other forms of so-called spiritual self-help.

What are crystals, and what is this so-called power or energy they are supposed to possess? Can crystals heal, improve psychic powers, act as "channels" to dead and disembodied spirits? How did such ideas arise, and what evidence is there to support such claims?

For two years, I have been searching for these answers, talking to believers, skeptics, writers, editors, geologists, crystal-shop owners, crystal "workers," and plain ordinary people who bought their own "personal" crystals to carry around with them. I have conducted scientific experiments, run surveys, performed computer literature searches, and bought, borrowed, and read dozens upon dozens of books on crystals and crystal power. In the process, I have written several articles and been interviewed by half a dozen magazines seeking answers to the riddle of "crystal power."

I don't know if I've found the "answer" to crystal power, but I do have a hypothesis—and plenty of scientific and statistical support for my hypothesis. I think I know what crystal power really is—and what it is not. As a materials-science student many years ago, I studied and worked with crystals all the time: performing x-ray diffraction studies, examining crystal structure under electron microscopes, growing large single crystals of germanium and silicon, measuring their electrical properties, even using piezoelectric quartz crystals to measure stress and strain in other metallic crystals. So, I think I have a fair feel for what crystals actually are and what "energies"—if any—they truly possess. I've used them, measured them, taken pictures of them, even written computer programs to simulate the effect of crystalline defects on crystal energies and properties.[2]

Hopefully, I bring more than just a scientific background in crystallography and materials science to this study of New Age crystal power. After spending eight years in college studying the science of crystals, I spent many more years studying and writing about esoteric subjects alleged to be "sciences": yoga, psychic phenomena, pyramids, the Bermuda Triangle, Atlantis, channeling, faith healing, voodoo, magic— and especially astrology.[3] I've practiced yoga, cast astrological charts, performed statistical studies of astrology and ESP, attended faith healings, watched in wonderment as the Amazing Randi performed "psychic surgery" not more than twenty feet from my unbelieving eyes, listened to experts lecture on flying saucers, ESP, poltergeists, and Bigfoot—all in the spirit of learning, trying to understand whether such mysteries and wonders can exist in our mundane, materialistic world filled with war, poverty, suffering, and environmental destruction.

Many of these mysteries I have come to understand, to

know how they fit into the fabric of the real world. Often, the real explanation is as marvelous as the esoteric explanation—if not as mysterious! Knowing how the Amazing Randi performs psychic surgery may not save me from cancer one day, but at least I won't be throwing away my last dollar and days on a worthless trip to the Philippines in search of a miracle cure. Knowing how astrologers and psychics can appear to make surprisingly accurate character readings and predictions may not make me a wealthy man, but at least I won't be squandering desperately short funds going to see Madame X—because I know I can cast fully as accurate a chart and make surprisingly accurate predictions on my own (as my editor will attest).

So I bring to this study of crystal power a wide range of scientific and esoteric knowledge. I have tried to put this knowledge to work while studying and experimenting with crystal power. As a scientist, I've had to be a skeptic—to doubt, to question, to put to the test, to see evidence and proof. As a seeker of esoteric knowledge, I've found myself "pulling for" the crystals, hoping for the experiments to come out in the crystals' favor—for my gas mileage to improve, for the crystal water to be purer and taste sweeter, for the crystal-water-fed plants to grow better, for my friends' headaches to go away, for the crystals to make me rich and famous.

After all, if I could find scientific evidence that crystal power actually exists, this book would find a ready and enthusiastic audience among the thousands, if not millions, of New Age practitioners, followers, and believers. I would probably have to find a new publisher for the book, but that small inconvenience would be far outweighed by tremendously increased sales—not to mention fame and acceptance among crystal workers and New Age followers. So, yes, I rooted for my crystals, thought good thoughts about them, caressed them, carried them about, cleansed them, "charged" them—in short, I did all the things the crystal workers said I should do to ensure success.

At each stage in the experiments, I recorded the intermediate results on my computer, carefully dating and documenting so there could be no doubt how each experiment was planned and carried out. Whenever possible, I took photographs to document further each step in the experiments and to provide proof of the results. Before I had written a single word of this book, I had built up a computer file 160K in size (half a disc) documenting research, experiments, and sources, all in addition to file folders inches thick plus entire shelves of library and personal books.

All of this study, experimentation, and documentation has been distilled into this book. I will try to separate the claims from the reality, outline the known history of crystal power and how it came into being, explain what crystals are and how they are formed, explain how science uses real crystal energies, then describe my own and others' experiments with crystals. Along the way, I will introduce my own hypothesis concerning crystal power and how it operates in the real world, how crystals can affect people, aid in the healing process, and serve as a "channel" to one's inner self.

Let the search for crystal power begin!

2

THE CLAIMS FOR
CRYSTAL POWER

The claims for crystal power run the gamut from modest to monstrous, from mundane to megaspiritual. One of the more modest claims made by all crystal workers and writers is that crystals possess an energy field extending one foot in all directions around the crystal. (Some say it is an electromagnetic field; others claim both an electromagnetic and bioplasmic field.) One of the more mundane claims is Dael Walker's assertion that attaching a crystal to the fuel line of a car's carburetor will improve gas mileage by 10% to 20%.[1] One might also consider mundane the claims that crystals can make you healthy, wealthy, and wise.

Among the more outlandish claims is that crystal power was used by the people of the lost continent of Atlantis to raise and place the huge blocks of stone used to build the Egyptian pyramids.[2] As for *mega*spirituality, few can beat the claims by Vicki and Randall Baer that "all Light, all Life, all Intelligence is coded crystallinity. . . . Quartz crystals and other precious stones are matrixed means by which the crystalline codes of personal and planetary consciousness are connectively interlinked with the higher Light-dimensions in an amplified, coherent manner. . . . Fundamentally, this is how creation works."[3]

Those of you who wear diamonds and precious stones as decorative jewelry may be dismayed to learn that crystals are "alive," and that spirits (called *cenoi* by shamans and "elementals" by some New Age writers) live within the faceted walls of your crystal jewelry. Even more dismaying, those same, innocent-looking stones are recording your every thought, your every deed, waiting for some crystal adept to come along and "unlock" your secrets!

Have you been suffering from acute headaches during the nights of the full moon? You must have a clear "masculine" quartz crystal (perhaps a rock crystal necklace or earrings) in your bedroom, because "a clear quartz crystal in the bedroom at the time of the full moon will cause all in the room to experience a great deal of painful pressure in the region of the crown of the head, pressure which subsides only when the offending crystal is removed from the room."[4]

Of all the claims for crystals and crystal power, the most difficult to fathom are those that cite ancient legendary civilizations which used crystals as their basic source of power, as tools for learning, communicating, recording, healing. Perhaps I could understand such claims being made for one or two, perhaps even three, legendary civilizations (Atlantis, Lemuria, and Mu come to mind), but why the crystal adepts insist on extending such claims to ever more mythical civilizations is beyond me. In addition to the three named, other legendary civilizations reportedly built upon crystal power include "the Cyclopeans (Els), Oraxians, Poseidans, anti-Atlanteans, Uramorans, and numerous others."[5]

Perhaps the crystal advocates feel there is safety in numbers, or that the bigger the lie, the more people will believe it, but for those of us trying to find some semblance of reality in the claims for crystal power, all these claims for mythical civilizations using crystals do little to convince and much to raise questions about the sanity of those who claim to know about Cyclopeans and Oraxians and Uramorans. Personally, I'd have to see a little physical evidence that Atlantis once existed (certainly the best known and most studied lost continent) before the others would take on much meaning.

Obviously, there is a huge gulf, a chasm of monstrous proportions, between the belief structure of crystal-power advocates and those of us who are still struggling with the concepts that crystals can transmit thought "energies" and help heal various diseases. Throughout this study of crystal power, I have sought to sift through the claims for those that appear reasonable, particularly for claims that are scientifically testable. Equally obviously, it's impossible to test the claim that the mythical people of Cyclops, Orax, or Uramor used crystals to power and build entire civilizations, which have somehow disappeared from the face of the earth, leaving no trace.

It's even difficult to test the seemingly straightforward claim that crystals can aid in the healing process—after all, drug companies invest millions of dollars in the controlled testing of a single new drug before the Federal Drug Administration (FDA) will approve its release on the market. However, as we shall see in Chapters 6 and 9, I do have a hypothesis about how crystals may help heal certain diseases and encourage people to feel better about themselves and their bodies—a hypothesis that *is* testable. Chapters 8 and 9 will look at this hypothesis and examine the evidence others and I have collected to support—or reject—it.

Other claims are much more testable, notably claims for the physical powers of crystals: that they can improve gas mileage, purify water, make plants grow faster and stronger. These claims have been put to the test in a series of carefully controlled experiments; detailed results are given in Chapter 9 and the Appendices.

For now, let's try to put the full range and scope of the claims for crystal power into perspective. At the beginning of this chapter, I labeled crystal-power claims as modest, mundane, monstrous, and megaspiritual. Perhaps a more useful classification would be: physical, medical, parapsychological, spiritual, and legendary. Using these categories, I have listed many dozens of claims for crystals assembled from a wide variety of sources: books, articles, interviews, and conversations.

Physical Claims for Crystal Power

- Crystals possess an energy field (electromagnetic and/or bioplasmic) extending a foot or so around the crystal.
- Crystals are alive.
- Natural crystals require thousands, or even millions, of years to grow.
- Crystals possess an "indwelling" elemental spirit *(cenoi)*.
- A quartz crystal attached to the fuel line of a car's carburetor (pointed toward the carburetor) will improve gas mileage.
- A quartz crystal placed in a jug of tap water will purify the water and make it taste sweeter.
- Such crystal-purified water will make plants grow faster and stronger.
- A quartz crystal placed next to a plant will help the plant grow faster and stronger.
- Quartz crystals can be "cleared" (made to appear clearer, that is, less cloudy) by a set ritual of cleansing and thought projection.
- A properly prepared and "programmed" crystal can make dreams and desires for riches, power, and love come true. This use of crystals is called "manifesting."
- A "programmed" quartz crystal placed under the pillow at night can "record" dreams and replay those dreams in the dreamer's mind when he or she wakes up.

Medical Claims for Crystal Power

- Crystals, especially quartz crystals, worn on approriate parts of the body can heal ailments and diseases affecting that part of the body.
- Crystals, especially quartz crystals, can serve as "channels" to amplify healing thoughts projected toward oneself or others.
- Crystals of different colors can heal body parts corresponding to those colors (e.g., green crystals improve eyesight).
- Crystals of different colors can cure certain diseases associated with those colors (e.g., red crystals stem blood flow and yellow crystals cure jaundice).
- Quartz crystals can activate the body's seven *chakras* (sensitive centers of spiritual energies, associated by some with the body's major glands: pineal, pituitary, thyroid, thymus, adrenals, pancreas, gonads); activated *chakras* will cure ailments associated with those *chakras*.
- Crystals, used in conjunction with herbs and a properly prescribed diet, can replace insulin injections for diabetics. (Unfortunately, I know of two patients who died.)
- Quartz and amethyst crystals attached to a dog's collar will heal wounds, vitalize listless dogs, and get rid of fleas.
- A crystal wand can help locate and cure muscle ailments in thoroughbred horses.

Parapsychological Claims for Crystal Power

- Crystals, particularly quartz crystals, improve and amplify ESP powers, especially telepathy (thought transmission between people).
- Quartz crystals act as "channeling amplifiers," improving communication with the dead, disembodied spirits, and "space brothers."
- Quartz crystal balls serve as "focusing screens" for long-distance viewing (clairvoyance) and foretelling the future (precognition).
- Quartz crystals improve one's power of clairaudience (the ability to "hear" the thoughts of others; some also claim to "hear" the dead talking, as well as spirits and/or "space brothers").

Spiritual Claims for Crystal Power

- Crystals can be used to communicate with God, Jesus, Buddha, and a host of "ascended masters."
- Each crystal has associated with it (and/or living within it) a spirit guide.
- Visualization techniques can be used to enlarge one's personal crystal to the size of a house, which can then be entered, whereupon the crystal worker can talk to God, Jesus, or other spirit guides.
- Crystal vibrations permit each person to attune to "God manifest in the perfection of crystal architecture."[6]

- Quartz crystals can activate and cleanse the body's seven *chakras,* opening up inspiration and communication to the "higher planes."
- Holding a quartz crystal near the heart will cleanse and activate the heart *chakra,* "the seat of the Spirit Self . . . to develop a measure of Christ Consciousness."[7]

Legendary Claims for Crystal Power

- Crystals were used by prehistoric shamans (medicine men) around the world to communicate with spirits and heal the sick. (Certainly, some prehistoric as well as modern shamans have used crystals.)
- Ancient Egyptians used crystals in their religious rituals.
- The pyramids of Egypt were once capped and/or faced with crystals.
- The lost civilization of Atlantis used huge 25-foot-high "power crystals" connected by copper rods as its primary power source.
- Legendary Atlanteans used natural crystals found in caves to cure the ill and counsel psychologically disturbed adolescents.
- Atlanteans made synthetic crystals used for healing, transportation, power, communication, etc.
- Atlanteans used crystals to make weightless the huge

blocks of stone used to construct the Egyptian pyramids.

- The lost civilizations of Lemuria and Mu (in the Pacific) likewise used huge "power crystals," as well as "knowledge crystals."
- When the continents of Atlantis, Lemuria, and/or Mu erupted and sank, survivors buried crystals containing the knowledge of their civilizations around the world, particularly in Arkansas, China, Mexico, Hawaii, and Peru.
- Survivors of the Atlantean civilization are said to have spread out across the world teaching Egyptians, Mayans, Incans, and North American Indians how to use crystals for spiritual power and healing.
- When the lost continent of Lemuria existed over a million years ago, huge "super crystals" (known as Earthkeepers) were used as custodians of ethereal planetary power and knowledge; one of these 500-pound super crystals was found in Arkansas in 1972, and has been moved to Hawaii and made the centerpiece of the San Marga Spiritual Sanctuary on Kauai.
- Other legendary civilizations using crystals include Cyclops (El), Orax, Poseidan, Uramor, and the anti-Atlanteans.

Quite an impressive list, isn't it? But by no means is it a complete list—nor an unrepresentative list; these are not even the most esoteric claims. (*Horoscope* magazine ran an article entitled, "Jewels of Enlightenment: An Esoteric Look

At Astrology and Gemstones" that may claim that distinction.[8]) Most of these claims can be found in any of several crystal books picked at random; many of the claims, particularly the spiritual and legendary claims, have been repeated over and over by almost all crystal-power advocates and authors.

For New Age crystal workers, three of the preceding claims are most important, forming the basis of modern crystal power:

1. Crystals can be programmed to "manifest" dreams and desires.
2. Crystals amplify and transfer healing thoughts (transference).
3. Crystals activate the body's *chakra* centers.

"Programming a crystal" is a term that needs some explaining: first, a crystal must be "cleansed" (usually by placing it in sea water or a clear running stream), then "cleared" of previous thought impressions (by holding the crystal and thinking, concentrating on the crystal appearing clearer); finally, the crystal is ready to be "programmed" with healing or "manifesting" thoughts (again, by holding the crystal and thinking, concentrating on the thought pattern with which you want the crystal to be programmed). The term *programming,* of course, is borrowed from the computer world, and the process of "programming a crystal" is considered to be much like programming a computer—except that you don't use a keyboard and your thoughts go directly into the crystal. (Computer programmers: Don't you wish it were that easy?)

The term *manifesting* refers to programmed thoughts and desires actually coming true in the real world: the desired check arrives in the mail or the desired companion comes into your life. Since crystals can be "programmed" with thought patterns, it comes as no surprise that crystals can also amplify and transfer those thought patterns to affect the behavior or health of others. Finally, since the New Age relies heavily on Eastern mysticism, it seems natural to add that crystals have an effect on the body's *chakra* centers (sensitive points in the body used by yogi adepts and acupuncturists). For instance, to get rid of a headache, hold a crystal above the head—pointing downward—and concentrate on activating the crown *chakra;* the crystal will amplify and transfer your thoughts, and soon a tingling will be felt in the crown of the head and the headache will disappear.

While these three claims form the basis for modern New Age crystal power, surprisingly, the idea that crystals are living things has gained considerable ground in recent years, based on the rather simple syllogism:

> Only living things can grow.
> Crystals grow.
> Therefore, crystals are alive.

True, we know today that crystals actually "grow" from source chemicals, given the right geological conditions of heat and pressure, or water seepage and evaporation. How *long* it takes a natural crystal to grow seems an open question but no doubt depends on environmental conditions; if volcanic magma cools rapidly, crystals can probably grow in a matter of hours or days, similar to synthetically grown crystals; under the processes of evaporation or sublimation, crystals would grow much more slowly, perhaps taking years or even hundreds of years—but thousands or millions of years as the crystal workers claim? Crystals grown at such a slow rate would probably lose their long-range order—in effect, new crystals would start growing so that the result would be many tiny crystallites, rather than a single, large crystal. Once a large crystal stops growing, it is very difficult to get it to start growing again; usually new crystals begin growing rather than the old one starting up again.

However fast the process, it is true that crystals do grow, but this hardly means they are alive! After all, storms can "grow," deserts can "grow"—even ideas can "grow." Crystals are no more alive than storms, a sandy sweep of desert, or ideas—at least in the biological sense of "alive." Today, artificial crystals can be grown in the laboratory under conditions simulating natural conditions deep within the earth. (Crystals are brought to the surface by the processes of mountain building, uplifting, and erosion.) The silicon and germanium crystals that form the substrate for the integrated circuits in our computers, TVs, and microwave ovens are grown by dipping a tiny seed crystal into molten silicon or germanium, then slowly drawing up the rotating seed and its growing cylindrical crystal; lengths of eighteen inches have been achieved. Growing such a crystal hardly qualifies one as a god creating a living thing! In fact, crystals grow simply because their symmetrical molecular arrangement is more energetically favorable than the noncrystalline liquid or gaseous state the chemical begins in.

One biochemist, Alexander Cairns-Smith, has even suggested that tiny quartz crystals in clay at the bottom of river beds were the original source of life on the planet (by growing and duplicating, along with attached amino acid molecules).[9] Oddly, the "crystals are alive" proponents fail to point out that diatoms, primitive algae that make up most of the plankton in the world's oceans, grow crystallike cell walls of silicon dioxide, the same chemical in quartz crystals and glass.

These, then, are some of the major (and minor) claims for crystal power; some seem harmless enough but others are so outrageous that it's hard to believe anyone considers them seriously, much less puts them down in black and white on the printed page—and gets paid!

We have briefly examined a few of these claims in this chapter: that crystals are alive because they grow, that crystals take millions of years to grow, that crystal power was used to build the pyramids. In succeeding chapters, all of the claims listed under all five categories—physical, medical, parapsychological, spiritual, and legendary—will be examined one by one in their appropriate context. Because the claims for crystal power are so varied and far-reaching, considerable background and context—historical, scientific, and medical— must be provided in order to understand fully what crystal power is and how it might function in our modern technological world.

Crystal-power advocates make dozens of incredible claims for their practice; I make only one claim for this book: that I will examine their claims and try to make some sense of them. In reading various other crystal power books and articles, it appears that the authors are vying with each other to achieve the most outrageous claims, to reach heights not yet scaled by their competitors. Sometimes, it seems there is almost nothing that crystals, especially quartz crystals, cannot do. Oddly enough, when you talk to these authors in person, they seem to come down to earth and the scale of their claims for crystal power lessens considerably, becoming almost reasonable.

For instance, I first talked to Dael Walker on the telephone before obtaining a copy of his *The Crystal Book*. After I posed a few questions about exactly how to obtain better gas mileage using a crystal, Dael realized I too was a writer and he opened up, describing a number of practical scientific tests of crystal power (several of which I have performed, as described in Chapter 9). Of all the crystal-power advocates I've talked to, Dael seemed the most reasonable, the most interested in good, solid scientific tests of crystal-power claims. Almost all the other crystal workers say the crystal "energies" lie outside the physical realm and thus cannot be detected or tested, that crystal power must be experienced and/or accepted on faith.

Imagine my surprise when I found Walker's *The Crystal Book* and read that he too has spirit guides and teachers inside his crystal to whom he talks, that he "channels" information about crystal use in Atlantis:

> The discovery of the use of crystals to control the incredible energy reaction beween matter and anti-matter gave birth to space flight. When they [Atlanteans] linked this drive to the ability of the crystal to assist the mind to travel inter-dimensionally, they were able to design interstellar space craft and fly to the stars. . . .
>
> Some of the priest-engineers talked to the deva spirits of the animal and vegetable kingdoms. With the deva's help they experimented to create new forms of life. Half vegetable, half animal, animals with wings or fish bodies were created. Some even merged animals and humans to create bird people, mermaids, minotaurs and centaurs. Nothing was impossible, for the crystal gave man dominion over the patterns of creation. They became like gods.[10]

Indeed, when it comes to crystal power it seems "Nothing was impossible," that crystals have (or had) the power to turn man into a god—when I would be satisfied just to improve my gas mileage!

3

THE HISTORY OF
CRYSTAL POWER

In Chapter 2 we looked at dozens of claims for crystal power; some of these claims have a long history stretching back thousands of years into prehistory and beyond. Modern proponents of crystal power love to cite its long and colorful history as proof that crystals do indeed have powers which we moderns have forgotten how to use. Historical claims for crystal power include:

- Prehistoric shamans used crystals as an essential part of their spiritual and medical practices.
- Shamans believed crystals were alive and/or that spirits (*cenoi*) lived within each crystal.
- Crystals were used by shamans and tribal chieftains in Australia, Siberia, Africa, North and South America, and Malaysia.
- A common shamanistic belief was that crystals were "thrown down from the heavens by the gods."

- Egyptians used crystals as an important part of their religious rituals.
- Egyptian pyramids were built with the aid of crystals.
- Egyptian pryamids were once capped and/or faced with crystals.
- Mayan priests used crystals and carved crystal skulls in their religious and sacrificial rites.
- North American Indians carried crystals in their medicine bags for healing purposes and put crystals on their eyelids to enhance dreams and their prophetic interpretations.
- During the Middle Ages, kings and queens had their crowns and other royal trappings bedecked with jewels to increase their power to rule.
- Likewise, the Catholic church—as well as other religious groups—placed jewels around the altar and on rings, crosses, scepters, and candlesticks.
- Wizards, magicians, and alchemists—even through the Renaissance—often used crystals as "power wands" and in combination with metals in their attempts to create gold and locate the famed philosopher's stone.
- Crystal gazing was practiced in ancient China, Japan, Greece, Rome, Arabia, and throughout the Middle Ages in Europe.

At first glance, such a list of the historical uses of crystals would seem to support the claim that crystal power has a long and illustrious history. Unfortunately, it's very difficult to judge the validity of the earlier claims—particularly the prehistoric shamanistic practices—and the later uses of jewels and crystals had much more to do with astrology and sympathetic magic than with New Age concepts of crystal power.

Certainly, shamans did use crystals in their healing ceremonies thousands of years ago. Given the beauty and symmetry of crystals, it would be surprising if they had not, but it's doubtful if shamanistic crystal power was as widespread as many modern writers proclaim. You can read half a dozen books on shamanism without coming across a single reference to crystals; shamans used many other artifacts they believed to be endowed with magical powers: herbs, feathers, water, parts of animals (bears were considered particularly powerful), shells, rocks, jade, pearls, and carvings (earth goddess carvings were common during Neolithic times)—almost anything rare or difficult to obtain. Viewed in this global perspective, crystals probably held little more power for ancient shamans than any other sacred object.

This is not to say that crystals did not play a role in early shamanism—only to question the extent and spread of prehistoric shamanistic use of crystals. Some evidence does exist: crystal pendants, probably worn as necklaces, have been unearthed from Neolithic sites (80,000 years ago), and an inscription on a 4000-year-old Babylonian cylinder seal reads, "A seal of Du-Shi-A (quartz crystal) will extend the possessions of a man and its name is auspicious."[1] While similar evidence of the use of crystals in prehistoric societies is scarce, the fact that shamans around the world—in Australia, Siberia,

Africa, and both South and North America—still use crystals today gives credence to the idea that crystal power was indeed an ancient esoteric art, providing a "bridge to the heavens."

Shamans consider crystals to be living rocks, thrown down by the gods from the firmament and thus linking the human and spirit worlds. Their belief that crystals were inhabited by *cenoi* and that those spirits could be cajoled into helping the shaman perform healings and other magical feats, can probably be traced as the source of the New Age belief that crystals can be used as "channels" to communicate with dead and disembodied spirits. Most New Age crystal advocates prefer to talk about crystal "energies" as the source of crystal power, but the ancient shamans who originated the idea of crystal power believed this power came from "indwelling" spirits; ancient shamans, of course, had no concept of modern electromagnetic or bioplasmic energies.

Most shamans—both ancient and present-day—have used crystals in much the same manner as witches and mystics use crystal balls, claiming to literally "see" the patient's illness inside the crystal with the aid of the *cenoi* spirit helpers believed to live within the stone.[2] Thus, shamanistic crystal power beliefs and practices can also be traced as the source of crystal gazing, also known as *scrying*. Crystal gazing will be discussed in detail later in this chapter.

Not all shamans use crystals in the traditional manner; one North American Indian tribe, the Southwestern Pomos, employs quartz crystals in a unique healing ceremony, which has more in common with psychic surgery than crystal gazing:

the Pomo "sucking doctor" sucks the pain from her stricken patient, then produces a quartz crystal from her mouth as proof that the pain has been removed.[3]

Other North American Indian tribes (Apache and Hopi) are said to have used crystals as an aid to dream visions and "spirit dreaming" (astral projection and communicating with the spirits) by placing quartz crystals on their eyelids before they went to sleep (presumably lying on their backs). The Cherokees are said to have believed that all history is recorded within clear quartz crystals,[4] a belief now linked by New Age crystal advocates to Atlantis and other legendary civilizations which supposedly possessed such "knowledge crystals."

Like ancient shamans, the Egyptians, too, probably used crystals in some of their rituals, but if the pyramids once were covered or capped with crystals it seems strange that no writer of the time mentioned that fact; for instance, Herodotus, who described many marvels in the ancient world and who visited the pyramids around 460 B.C., makes no mention of crystals on or atop the pyramids in his *History,* although he does describe the crystal coffins used by the Ethiopians to display their dead. Books on Egyptian art and museums are strangely devoid of any samples of ceremonial crystals—although a necklace or two containing quartz crystals are pictured—so it's unlikely that crystals played much of a role in Egyptian society.

As for the claim that survivors from Atlantis went to Egypt and used crystals to build the pyramids, I would merely point to the scientific studies demonstrating that contemporary materials and techniques—plus thousands of slaves—were quite capable of cutting, transporting, and lifting into place the huge stones used to construct the pyramids. I'm sure the Egyptian slaves would have been quite happy to have some Atlantean wizard do their back-breaking labor for them!

During the Middle Ages in Europe, wizards and magicians were wont to use crystals on their magic wands, while the many jewels adorning the crowns of kings and queens were supposed to increase their "cosmic energy," turning the king into "a living battery of power for the nation."[5] However, the medieval affinity for jewels and precious stones should *not* be taken as evidence of or support for crystal power; the alleged power of gems had much more to do with their *color* than with any crystal power "energies." In fact, astrology played an important role in the popularity of precious stones during the Middle Ages, since each sign of the zodiac was assigned a particular "ruling" stone, usually based on its color. For instance, the red bloodstone was assigned to Aries, ruled by the red planet Mars (rubies were also associated with Mars), while the yellow jacinth was assigned to Leo, ruled by the sun.[6]

As I explain in *Astrology Disproved,* this association between a planet's color and its alleged influence is one aspect of sympathetic magic, also known as the principle of correspondences (objects with similar qualities can influence each other).[7] Although some New Age crystal workers include astrology in their cosmology, very few link crystal power with astrology and sympathetic magic; for most, the clear quartz crystal is the only stone with real power, although the amethyst (a type of quartz) does run a poor second and tourmaline a distant third in popularity. In fact, clear quartz was rarely mentioned by medieval astrologers as having any strong powers or associations, although other medieval magicians and alchemists did use quartz in their power wands and for scrying.

Scrying, or crystal gazing, seems to be the closest the Middle Ages ever got to any modern concept of crystal power. In his famous book, *The Curious Lore of Precious Stones,* George Kunz presents the results of his life-long study of crystal gazing:

> The points of light reflected from the polished surface (*points de repere*) serve to attract the attention of the gazer and to fix the eye until, gradually, the optic nerve becomes so fatigued that it finally ceases to transmit to the sensorium the impression made from without and begins to respond to the reflex action proceeding from the brain of the gazer. In this way the impression received from within is apparently projected and seems to come from without. It is easy to understand that the results must vary according to the idiosyncrasy of the various scryers; for everything depends upon the sensitiveness of the optic nerve. In many cases the effect of prolonged gazing upon the brilliant surface will simply produce a loss of sight, the optic nerve will be temporarily paralyzed and will as little respond to stimulation from within as from without; in other cases, however, the nerve will be only deadened as regards external impressions, while retaining sufficient activity to react against a stimulus from the brain centres. It is almost invariably stated that, prior to the appearance of the desired visions, the crystal seems to disappear and a mist rises before the gazer's eye.[8]

In short, Kunz, a scientist and curator at the American Museum of Natural History, felt that crystal gazers really do see visions, produced by the physiological effects of staring at a fixed point within the crystal ball; the visions themselves are projected by the brain (subconscious or unconscious mind?) of the gazer. Another writer, Andrew Lang, attributed the crystal images to "hypnagogic illusions—images which appear when the eyes are closed and before sleep supervenes."[9]

Whatever the source of the crystal images, they provide us with a clue to the source of another crystal-power belief: that spirits live within crystals. Many gazers "saw" spirits, usually evil spirits, within crystal balls, mirrors, and even on the surface of water:

> The power to see images of evil spirits on the surface of water was claimed by those called *hydromantii* in the ninth century. This is attested in a work composed about 860 A.D. by Hinemar, archbishop of Rheims, who characterized the supposed appearances as "images or deceptions of the demons." These diviners asserted that they received audible communications from the spirits and they therefore evidently believed that the appearances were realities.[10]

Thus, in crystal gazing, we see the beginnings of several of the ancient and modern claims for crystal power:

- Spirits live within crystals.
- Crystals can serve as channels for spirit communications.

- Crystals can serve as the focus for visualization techniques.

While I realize that many people—in fact most people—believe in some form of life after death, believe that we survive passage from this earthly coil in a spirit form of one kind or another, I would point out that we have no scientific evidence for the existence of any kind of spirits—dead, disembodied, or the outer-space variety. Not even Houdini, whose study of spiritualism was rivaled by none, has been able to send through a message from the "other side" since his death. (One spiritualist did claim to receive a predetermined code, but he was shown to have had prior access to the secret message through Houdini's wife.)

Most scientific writers on the subject say there is no *theoretical* basis in our modern physics and biology for survival of a spirit or soul. This is not quite so; the physics of chemistry makes use of a mysterious mathematical function called *entropy*, which is a measure of disorder in the universe (the more disorder, the higher the entropy). If there exists a type of entropy associated with life (that is, if living creatures have a higher negative entropy simply because they are alive), I can imagine a type of survival after death in the form of entropy wave-fields. Unfortunately for those who see and talk to spirits inside crystals, entropy is not a *physical* quantity; it cannot be seen or measured directly, only indirectly. (If this sounds like crystal bioplasmic energies, you're right; more on this in Chapter 8.)

In short, entropy does not exist in real space and time,

only within a mathematical and theoretical framework. Thus, even if something we could term "entropy spirits" did exist, we would only be able to have contact via our own "entropy fields." We certainly would not be able to see or hear or talk to them. Note also that, because crystals are highly ordered structures, they too contain a high degree of negative entropy. But how could a highly negative "entropy spirit" live inside a crystal? (Entropy naturally "flows" from high negative to high positive, so that the universe is always running down, that is, it is becoming more disordered.)

So, even on a wildly theoretical basis, I'm afraid there is very little chance a spirit could live within a crystal, much less carry on spiritual dissertations or provide secret knowledge about legendary civilizations.

Of course, ancient shamans knew nothing about entropy or bioplasmic energy; they had to invent spirits in order to awe their subjects and clients, to convince them that they, the shamans, did indeed have the power to heal, to see the future. How better to awe and convince the already super-stitious than to claim direct contact with the spirits? Everybody knew it was beyond ordinary powers to heal, to see the future; only mysterious spirits could do that.

Modern shamans, even those who don't use crystals, do exactly that: they claim to be able to cajole, manipulate, and control the evil spirits causing the illness. In his excellent study of East Indian shamans, Sudhir Kakar writes: "There are many practicing sorcerers called *sayanas* (wise; cunning) who cater to a large clientele. These *sayanas* perform the healing function of casting out demons in addition to going about the 'proper' occult tasks—'to command the presence of the Jinn and demons who, when it is required of them, cause anything to take place; to establish friendship or enmity between two persons; to cause the death of an enemy; to increase wealth or salary; to gain income gratuitously or mysteriously; to secure the accomplishment of wishes, temporal or spiritual.' "[11]

Note the similarity between the claims of what an East Indian shaman can do and the claims for crystal power. The only differences are that an East Indian shaman does not use a crystal, and most modern crystal workers would deny that demons are responsible for the power of their crystals to grant wishes. (They might admit to a good spirit, but never an evil spirit.)

Thus, we see that many of the claims for crystal power are borrowed from shamanism, regardless of whether or not crystals are involved.

As we saw in Chapter 2, modern crystal workers call the granting of wishes and desires "manifesting." Most use visualization techniques to "program" their crystal for "manifesting." In *The Crystal Book,* Dael Walker describes how to use visualization techniques to "manifest" a new car:

> Get in a comfortable position. Hold your crystal in your left hand. Close your eyes. See your crystal in front of you with the point up. See it getting larger and larger until it is as large as a house. There is a door open. Go inside. Once again, look around you. Look at the light coming through the ceiling and shining on the walls and floor. Smell the odor of the crystal.

Listen to the special sound. Taste the crystal. Feel the temperature. Touch the walls and feel the surface.

Walk over to the doorway which says "Manifesting Room." Walk into the room and look around. The walls are solid gold. The floor is green. The ceiling is studded with millions of precious gemstones, sparkling with all the colors of the rainbow. The room is filled with a warm feeling of total prosperity.

If you are manifesting a new car, bring the image of the car into the manifesting room. Look at it carefully and see that it is the right color, interior, model and make. Be sure it has all the right accessories such as radio, air conditioning, stereo cassette, sun roof, coffee maker, sauna, hot tub, pool, or whatever you want.

Open the door and sit down in the driver's seat. Feel the cushions settle, put your feet on the pedals, check the lights, blow the horn and smell the new smell inside. Let all your senses be aware of the whole car. Now, reach inside the glove compartment and pull out the receipt with your name on it marked PAID IN FULL. Take the receipt, put it in your pocket

Figure 3-1: Crystal Power Manifesting; This Car's for You!

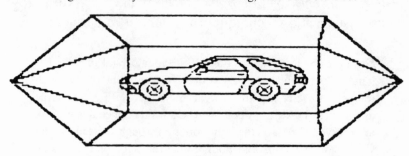

and say out loud, "This is mine; I own it: it belongs to me." Say this three times with as much feeling and acceptance as you can. End the manifesting with the statement, "In all I create, let Divinity be my guide." Now, come out of the manifesting room, step out of your crystal and back into your body. When you feel comfortable, open your eyes.

Do this twice a day for 33 days.[12]

Imagine: only twice a day, for thirty-three days and, *voilà,* a new car, complete with sauna and pool! Stupid me. I paid $205 a month for four years for a simple pickup truck with no sauna and no pool!

4

THE NATURAL SCIENCE
OF CRYSTALS

When most people think of crystals, they think of jewels: diamonds, rubies, rock crystals—hard, glasslike objects with flat, symmetrical surfaces and sharp corners and edges. However, crystals come in many different forms, shapes, and growth patterns. We use crystals all the time, often without knowing it. The salt and sugar on our table are tiny cubic crystals, readily soluble in water. Under a low-power microscope, salt and sugar crystals appear in a dizzying array of sizes and shapes: crystals growing on top of crystals, some crystals growing as nearly perfect cubes, others with angular sides and facets, often many tiny crystals growing attached in clusters. Yet, to the naked eye, sugar and salt appear as tiny grains, bare motes of white dust.

The naked eye will also fail to see another form of crystal sitting right next to our sugar and coffee cup—the metal spoon! Few people realize that all metals are crystalline as well, though rarely will they form into the regular symmetrical shapes we associate with crystals. Most metal crystals are very tiny, with irregular growth patterns, called *crystallites*. Very rarely will metals occur as single crystals but rather as an amalgam of thousands of tiny crystallites joined together at grain boundaries. As metals solidify from the melt, many hundreds and thousands of tiny crystals begin growing simultaneously; as they grow, they rapidly run into each other in all three directions, thus forming grain boundaries between the jumble of crystallites.

In fact, one of the major reasons metals are so *weak* is because they are *not* single crystals; the bond between atoms at the grain boundaries is much weaker than the bond between atoms within good crystal structure, so metals have a tendency to fail along grain boundaries and other imperfections, which is why metal-fatigue breaks appear very jagged and rough. Even within the single-crystal areas, metals contain many imperfections which weaken the strength of the crystal, so that normal tensile breaks in metals occur not along grain boundaries but across single crystallites. Nearly perfect (defect-free) single crystals of iron have been grown as very thin whiskers; their strength is nearly ten thousand times that of ordinary iron crystals.

What are crystals? Why are some so incredibly strong while others (like talc) crumble to the touch? Why do some crystals form such regular, symmetrical shapes, while others grow in a mishmash of irregular shapes and patterns?

The answer, in a word, is *energy*—not the mysterious bioplasmic energy cited by crystal-power advocates, but the very real energy of atomic bonding. Put simply, most inorganic elements and compounds form crystals because the close-packed atomic patterns of crystals are energetically more favorable than the random packing of the amorphous noncrystalline state. As atoms and molecules are added to the growing crystal, the heat energy of formation is lowest, and thus more favorable, when the atoms and molecules situate themselves at certain distances and angles from the atoms and molecules already part of the crystal. Scientists think of this energy-positioning process as a sort of three-dimensional "energy well" (see Figure 4–1); when atoms and

Figure 4–1: Energy Well determines most favorable distance
between molecules in a crystal

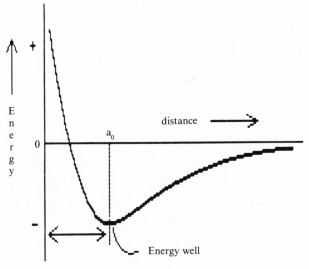

a_0 is most favorable distance between molecules in crystal

molecules align themselves at the proper distances and angles, they fall into the bottom of this energy well and become locked into place.

Crystal Growth

This three-dimensional, molecular-bonding process has distinct limits to the different kinds of crystals that can be produced (that is, grown). In 1850, a French mathematician, Auguste Bravais, demonstrated that only fourteen crystal *groups* are theoretically possible, for a total of thirty-two different crystal *classes,* which can be further classified in one of six crystal *systems,* depending on the angles and lengths of crystal axes (see Chart 4–1). Crystal class determines the basic shape of a crystal, although the final external shape we see may not resemble the unit cell because of uneven growth rates of different sides.

The question, then, "What is a crystal?" has a rather complex answer—but not a mysterious one. Remember, it has taken hundreds of years for scientists and mathematicians to figure out the internal structure of crystals and how they are formed. Chart 4–1 presents the basic scientific information about crystals and how they grow, but that is just scratching the surface. To understand crystals—particularly natural crystals—requires years and decades of study. Yet after a few months or years of holding and meditating over a few purchased quartz crystals, their advocates claim to understand

CHART 4–1: What Is a Crystal?

Solid: There are two types of solids: crystalline and amorphous (glasses). Crystalline solids have regular, repetitive three-dimensional molecular structures. All minerals and metals are crystalline, composed of thousands of tiny crystals wedged together at grain boundaries; only a few minerals form the familiar, large single crystals, such as quartz (silicon dioxide in hexagonal crystals) and diamonds (carbon in tetrahedral crystals). Amorphous or noncrystalline solids are sometimes referred to as "solid liquids," because their molecules are so tangled in the liquid state that they cannot untangle and form crystalline solids. Common examples are plastics and glass.

Symmetrical: Because crystals grow (at the rate of 16 trillion atoms per hour) in regular, repeated three-dimensional patterns, they contain one or more of three types of symmetry: (1) *plane of symmetry,* which can be divided into two halves that are mirror images; (2) *axis of symmetry,* which can be rotated two, three, four, or six times so that the crystal looks the same as at the start; (3) *center of symmetry,* which is any line through the center intersecting opposite faces at equal distances.

Systems of crystals: All crystals fall into one of thirty-two classes of crystals, which can be further classified in one of six crystal systems:

Isometric: all 90° angles, equal-length axes: cubic and octahedral crystals (salt [halite], fool's gold, diamond).

Tetragonal: all 90° angles, 2 equal-length axes (cristobalite [a type of quartz], rutile [titanium oxide]).

Orthorhombic: all 90° angles, unequal-length axes (sulphur, barite [barium sulphate], topaz).

Monoclinic: angle greater than 90°, unequal-length axes (gypsum, mica, talc, hornblende).

Triclinic: no 90° angles, unequal-length axes (orpiment [arsenic sulphide], axinite).

Hexagonal: 60° angles, horizontal axes equal (quartz, calcite, tourmaline).

Growth: crystals that we find or buy grow in one of five ways:

Crystallization from molten material: as volcanic magma cools, metals and gem crystals crystallize from the melt.

Sublimation: hot volcanic gases pass over cool surfaces and deposit crystals of sulphur, fluorite, halite, etc.

Evaporites from water solution: in arid, desert regions, water containing dissolved minerals evaporates and leaves crystals known as evaporites; can also occur in underground caves and openings.

Metamorphism: earth shifts and volcanic pressures can change the crystalline structure of existing rocks and minerals.

Weathering: acidic water chemically attacks and changes minerals.

crystals and their properties better than the gemologist.

Figure 4–2 shows two of the most common types of crystals, isometric cubic and hexagonal; note how a single *unit cell,* consisting of six or more atoms of the appropriate types situated at precise three-dimensional locations, defines what the crystal looks like and how it will grow—even though a large crystal will consist of trillions of atoms, all more or less lined up in the same relative angles and distances. Because millions and trillions of atoms must be added to a crystal's surface as it grows, the chances of defects—imperfections in the crystal lattice—are very high; even the most perfect appearing diamond or quartz crystal will contain thousands of several different kinds of defects:

Figure 4–2: Unit cells determine basic crystal structure

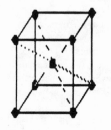

body-centered cubic unit cell

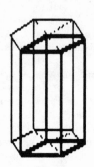

simple hexagonal unit cell

- Point defects: missing atoms (holes) and impurities.
- Line defects: misaligned planes of atoms meet along a line (dislocation).
- Three-dimensional defects: (1) stacking faults: entire plane of atoms is "missing" or stacked in the wrong order; (2) twinning: crystal starts growing as a mirror image of itself.

As we shall see in Chapter 5, modern scientists, engineers, and technicians require crystals as perfect as possible to perform their electronic wizardry; in fact, most of the crystals we now use are man-made, created under carefully controlled conditions in the laboratory, because naturally grown crystals are not pure or perfect enough. Some, like the large silicon and germanium single crystals that form the substrates for our computer chips, never occur in nature. Even the most valuable gems can now be synthesized in the laboratory: diamonds, rubies, sapphires, and, of course, quartz.

Yet, crystal-power advocates insist that only natural crystals grown by Mother Earth can be used for crystal-power work—in spite of the fact that natural crystals are far less likely to be free of defects. Should not a more perfect crystal amplify and transmit crystal power energies more efficiently, just as science finds that electronic devices require near-perfect crystals? What does this tell us about the nature of the so-called bioplasmic or orgone "energy" supposedly used by crystal workers?

Crystals in Nature

All of the thirty-two classes of crystals are represented by crystals grown in nature, although some classes (cubic, hexagonal) are more common in the crystals we find. The natural quartz so favored by crystal workers is but one of five natural forms of silicon dioxide (SiO_2), three of which are crystalline and two amorphous:

- Cristobalite, SiO_2: cubic or tetragonal.
- Lechatelierite, SiO_2: amorphous.
- Opal, $SiO_{2}{}_{x}H_2O$: amorphous.
- Tridymite, SiO_2: rhombic.
- Quartz, SiO_2: hexagonal.

Quartz, considered the most common and widespread mineral, is found in nature in a wide variety of forms: colorless rock crystal favored by crystal-power advocates, rose quartz (color due to traces of manganese), amethyst (color also due to traces of manganese), smoky quartz (color due to radium activity), plus another whole set of minerals called *cryptocrystalline quartz* (with microscopic crystals), including flint, jasper, agate, and onyx.

In short, crystals in nature come in a wide variety of chemical compounds, crystal structures, and mineral forms. Which form a particular chemical will take depends on conditions: availability of source material, temperature, pressure, impurities, presence or absence of water, rate of growth, rate of cooling, etc. Given the right conditions and source chemicals—molten magma, dissolved chemicals, or hot chemical gases—particular types of crystals and minerals will form. In theory, given the chemicals and conditions, the scientist can predict what crystals will form; in fact, he does just that in the laboratory when he makes synthetic crystals.

There is no magic, no mysterious process at work, when a crystal is formed. Clear quartz rock crystal is formed when silicon ions and oxygen ions come together under the right conditions of temperature and pressure; under different conditions, other types of quartz or crystalline forms of silicon dioxide will be created.

What makes natural, clear quartz crystals different from any other natural or synthetic crystal? It is true that good, clear quartz crystals are rarer than other types of quartz but otherwise they differ little from the darker varieties. Many other types of crystals—cubic halite, tetragonal rutile, orthorhombic sulfur, for instance—grow as large, well-formed single crystals. Why is quartz considered so different, so special, by crystal-power advocates? The same chemical and thermodynamic forces work to create quartz crystals as any other type of crystal. What could possibly happen in nature to give clear quartz crystals any special powers or energies we humans can tap into merely by thinking?

All minerologists and gem collectors I've talked to say such crystal energies do not exist, that they've never sensed anything different about quartz crystals despite decades of hunting, collecting, and handling the stones. Crystal-power advocates would retort, "That's because they aren't *attuned* to the crystals."

By being attuned, crystal-power advocates are referring to the use of quartz crystals as oscillators, clocks, and radio receivers. Chapter 5 will look at the electromagnetic properties of crystals—particularly quartz crystals—and how they are used to create electronic and other high-tech gadgetry.

5

ELECTROMAGNETISM: MODERN USES OF CRYSTALS

Ever since prehistoric man began scraping rocks, flint, and obsidian to shape tools and create fire, crystals have been a part of our technology. With the discovery of metals and metal working, crystals—in the form of amalgams of thousands of tiny crystallites—launched man on the road to modern technology. Roman soldiers may not have cared that their steel swords and bronze drinking cups were composed of crystals, but certainly metals accelerated the growth and spread of civilization, while the larger, more obvious crystals such as quartz and diamond remained decorative and/or sacred objects of art.

With the discovery of electricity, and its relationship to that most peculiar of forces, magnetism, the stage was set for these formerly decorative gems to add to the civilization

CHART 5–1: Modern Uses of Crystals

Radios, TVs: Thin slices of quartz crystals are used as frequency-tuning devices because they oscillate at precise electronic frequencies, ranging from thousands of cycles per second (AM frequencies) to millions of cycles per second (FM and TV frequencies). This crystal oscillation occurs in asymmetric crystals because they are *piezoelectric:* electrical fields cause mechanical strains and deformations. Placed in an oscillating circuit, these tuning crystals select the precise frequency wanted, which is then amplified so we can see or hear the broadcast.

Integrated circuits: Specially grown single crystals of silicon or germanium six inches in diameter are sliced into thin wafers; the microscopic circuitry is then etched and deposited on this wafer substrate using photolithography techniques. The fact that the wafers are crystals has little to do with the operation of integrated circuits; the wafer substrates must be single crystals to provide uniform semiconducting properties so that the thousands of tiny transistors manufactured through photolithography will behave in a predictable uniform manner.

Sonar devices: Piezoelectric crystals not only produce an electrical field when mechanically deformed, but the reverse process also takes place: when an electrical field is applied to such crystals, they contract or expand accordingly—*converse piezoelectricity*. Thus, plates of quartz crystals can be used to detect and transmit underwater sound waves.

Strain gauges: Piezoelectric crystals such as quartz can also be used as strain gauges to detect minute strains and deformations in metals; as the metal deforms, the strain gauge (again, a thin slice of quartz crystal) produces a corresponding electrical current that tells the researcher how much strain and deformation has taken place.

Pressure gauges: Using the same principle as in strain gauges, piezoelectric crystals can also be used as pressure gauges.

Temperature sensors: Some piezoelectric crystals are also *pyroelectric:* changes in temperature produce an electrical field across the crystal, which in turn produces a current that can be used to measure the temperature change. Quartz is somewhat pyroelectric, but tourmaline has the strongest pyroelectrical properties.

Nonelectrical uses: Quartz and related minerals are also used in enormous tonnages in the construction and manufacturing industries: as building stone, as an aggregate in concrete, as sand in mortar and cement, as a flux in metallurgy, in the manufacture of glass and ceramics, as an abrasive, and as an inert filler.

of the industrial era, the information age. Chart 5–1 lists some of the modern uses of crystals we will examine in this chapter. Most of those uses involve the electromagnetic properties of crystals, which began to be discovered barely more than a century ago.

In 1880, the Curie brothers, Jacques and Pierre, discovered that quartz crystals subjected to pressure became weak "batteries," developing positive and negative electrical charges at

Figure 5–1: Piezoelectric crystals convert mechanical vibrations into AC voltage; converse effect also occurs.

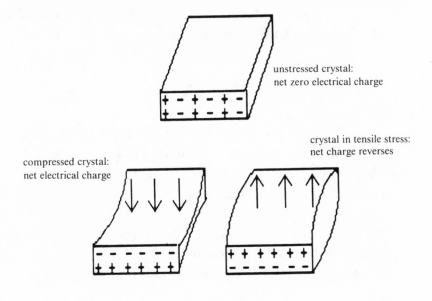

unstressed crystal:
net zero electrical charge

crystal in tensile stress:
net charge reverses

compressed crystal:
net electrical charge

opposite ends of certain axes. This effect, a material developing an electrical charge as a result of mechanical pressure, is called *piezoelectricity;* such materials, especially quartz, also show the opposite effect, becoming mechanically deformed when subjected to an electrical field (the *converse piezoelectric effect*).[1] Figure 5-1 illustrates the piezoelectric effect and its converse.

Engineers and scientists think of piezoelectric crystals as *transducers,* transforming electrical energy into mechanical energy, and vice versa. Later in this chapter, we shall see how laser crystals also transform energy from one form into another (light, electrical, or chemical energy to monochromatic light). Piezoelectricity is a very real, physical effect; electrically excited crystals physically vibrate, and mechanically strained crystals physically put out a measurable electrical current.

Crystal Oscillators

Piezoelectricity was put to good use in the early 1900s when the crystal radio-receiver set was invented in 1906. In fact, crystals—usually galena, lead sulfide, or quartz—were used in several different ways in early radios:

- As the frequency-selection component of frequency-detection circuits (galena, quartz);
- As the sound-producing component of earphones (mica, quartz); and
- As feedback control oscillators (galena).

Figure 5-2: Piezoelectric Quartz Crystal in Earphone
photo by Lawrence Jerome

Thus, a crystal radio may use both piezoelectric principles: a slice of quartz crystal acting as a tuning resonator, selecting the precise frequency we want to hear, while a second crystal slice in the earphone acts as the loudspeaker when the selected frequency is transmitted to it. Figure 5–2 shows a photograph of a piezoelectric quartz crystal used in an earphone.

The most important use of a crystal in a radio is in frequency selection, and in helping to maintain that frequency against unwanted "drift." Changes in temperature are the main source of drift, and since crystals have a near-zero temperature coefficient, they provide a good, steady lock on a particular frequency. Crystals detect frequency when their mechanical vibration rate matches the incoming AC voltage-excitation frequency: the crystal begins to vibrate at its natural frequency (converse piezoelectric effect), in turn generating an AC voltage of that same frequency (piezoelectric effect). However, if the incoming voltage frequency is just a little different from the crystal's natural oscillation frequency, little mechanical vibration occurs and, hence, little piezoelectric voltage is produced (see Figure 5–3). The actual frequency selected depends on the thickness of the crystal: the thinner the crystal, the higher the frequency selected.[2]

Figure 5–3: Piezoelectric quartz crystals oscillate
at vibrational resonant frequency

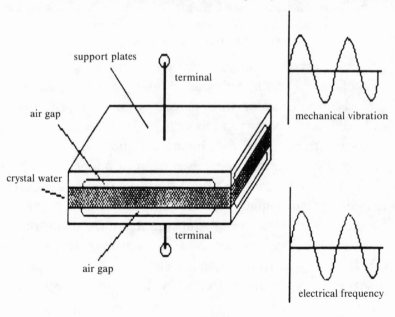

Oddly enough, crystal-power advocates recommend careful selection of a crystal; they suggest you hold different crystals in your hand until one has the right feel, the right vibration. Are they subjectively (subconsciously) sensing some vibration (I certainly have never felt the tingle they describe), or are they somehow mentally "tuning in" to that particular crystal's natural vibrational frequency? Chapter 7, "The Power of the Mind," attempts to analyze this question, comparing the mind's natural vibration frequencies (approximately 3 to 300 cycles per second) with the vibration frequency of crystals (millions of cycles per second).

During World War I, piezoelectric quartz crystals were tested for transmitting and detecting submarine sound waves. The same principle of converse piezoelectricity has been used for decades of metallurgical research by attaching thin slices of quartz crystals to metal under strain and measuring the electrical output of such strain gauges—the higher the electrical output, the higher the strain.

Today, synthetic quartz crystals are used as precisely oscillating clocks to time the operations of our computers, at rates from 4.7 megahertz (4.7 million cycles per second) to 40 megahertz (40 million cycles per second). Without such precise timing, computers would have difficulty communicating with peripheral devices and other computers. And, of course, most of our clocks and watches today are timed by oscillating quartz crystals; some of these cheaper digital timepieces contain crystals that do not vibrate at the proper frequency and will run either slower or faster than they should. (I have one that gains a half-minute a day with unerring accuracy!)

Computer Chips

Without a doubt, the most important contribution crystals make to the modern information age are the single-crystal substrates upon which all of our sophisticated integrated circuits are constructed. Before any of the circuitry is created, computer chips begin as thin slices (wafers) of single-crystal silicon or germanium, properly "doped" with impurities to turn the normally insulating silicon or germanium into a semiconductor (electrical fields produce small electrical currents). These single crystals of silicon and germanium are not found in nature, but are grown in the laboratory by literally pulling the crystal from the melt: a tiny seed crystal is suspended on a rotating shaft above the molten material, then slowly lowered to touch the liquid surface; once crystal growth has begun, the seed is raised, still rotating, while a cylindrical single crystal grows beneath, widening in diameter as it is pulled up until maximum diameter is reached. A few hours later, a near perfect cylindrical single crystal of silicon or germanium, five or six inches in diameter and at least as long, hangs suspended from the puller, ready to be sliced and imprinted with the intricate circuitry that will create as many as a hundred tiny integrated circuits (chips) on a single wafer.

Unfortunately for the crystal-power advocates who point to this use of crystals in our computer chips as evidence that crystals do indeed possess the ability to be programmed, the fact that the substrates are single crystals has little to do with the operations of the integrated circuits later constructed on their surface. Single crystals of silicon and germanium are used as chip substrates because their electrical properties are *isotropic* (the same in all directions) along the axis of slicing; in short, integrated circuits are built on single-crystal wafers so that the thousands of tiny transistors spread out over an area of one-inch square or less will all operate the same (e.g., switch at the same voltage levels).

Single-crystal wafer substrates contribute only uniformity to the electrical operation of integrated circuits; the actual electronic circuitry depends on the overlaying circuit design created by a complex series of processes (photolithography, masking, etching, and chemical-vapor deposition).

None of the properties of crystals we have discussed (piezoelectricity, frequency oscillation) play a role in the operation of computer chips.

Today, as many as 20,000 transistors can be placed on a single integrated circuit "die"; each one of those tiny transistors is an analogue of the familiar large vacuum tubes once found inside our radios and TVs. Operationally, the only difference is that vacuum tubes required much higher voltages and electrical currents; the typical integrated circuit transistor operates within a voltage range of .1 to .6 millivolts, thousands of times less than the old-fashioned vacuum tubes. Integrated circuits generate far less heat and last far longer than vacuum tubes—and take up far less room—but they are no more an example of crystal power than the obsolete vacuum tube.

Lasers, however, present a different situation. In many

respects, the modern use of crystals as lasers *does* parallel the type of energy transfer claimed for crystal power: one form of energy—light, electricity, chemical energy—is transformed by the crystal into another—light of a particular frequency. Piezoelectricity also transforms energy from one form to another, but the mechanical response of the crystal remains localized: the crystal vibrates, affecting the air around it to produce sound, but otherwise not transmitting that mechanical energy any great distance—certainly not enough to raise building blocks for the pyramids!

Lasers, then, are our best physical analogy to the sort of energy transfer claimed for crystal power: that crystals transform mental and emotional "energies" into some mysterious "crystal energy," which is stored and/or amplified and then transmitted directly to those who are "attuned." Other crystal advocates claim that the mental/emotional energies and the crystal energies are really one and the same bioplasmic or orgone energy. However, most crystal-power advocates claim that crystals can do *physical* things, such as improve one's gas mileage or lift fifty-ton blocks of rock; hence, some portion of crystal "energy" must be physical in nature. In order for an Atlantean crystal worker to lift fifty tons of rock merely by pointing a quartz crystal at it and thinking, "Rise, stone," the crystal must transform the mental thought-patterns, RISE STONE, into some physical (gravitational?) energy.

To see how crystals transform energy from one form into another, let's look closer at how a laser operates.

Crystal Lasers

While it's true that the first laser was a crystal—a ruby crystal polished and mirrored at both ends—the fact that it was a crystal had little to do with its laser light-producing capabilities. Since that first crystal laser in 1960, lasers have been made from a wide variety of substances: gases, liquids, and non-crystalline solids. Obviously, if gases and liquids can *lase* (a verb invented by laser scientists to indicate a material's ability to produce laser radiation), crystallinity can have little to do with the phenomenon; in fact, *impurities* in the ruby crystal—chromium atoms replacing the aluminum atoms in the crystal aluminum oxide structure—act as the source of the red laser light. The impurities don't need to be in a crystal structure at all; glass "doped" with the right impurities will also "lase."

The term *laser* stands for "light amplification by stimulated emission of radiation." Individual atoms are stimulated (excited to a higher energy level), not the entire crystal as in the case of the piezoelectric effect. Electrons in an atom do not orbit the nucleus at just any distance or energy level, but are constrained to particular distances and energy levels. When an electron is excited to a higher energy level, it absorbs a particular amount of energy; any additional energy is given off as light or heat. When such an excited atom decays to a lower energy level, it emits a bundle of electromagnetic energy—a photon of a particular frequency, as shown in Figure 5-4.

Figure 5–4: Excited atoms emit radiation which stimulates more laser light

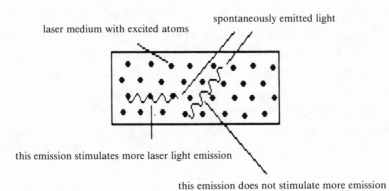

Lasers can produce a broad spectrum of electromagnetic radiation, ranging from microwaves (the longest wavelength, .001 meters) to X-rays (the shortest laser wavelength, .000000001 meters), including of course visible light at the middle of the spectrum (10^{-6} to 10^{-7} meters). To produce a laser beam, the object is to get as many of the impurity atoms excited as possible (the scientists call this a population inversion), which then all decay (emit radiation) in a very short period of time, emitting a brief, powerful coherent beam of light lasting a bare billionth of a second to a tenth of a second. Continuous laser beams can also be created by restimulating decayed atoms, or by continuously replacing decayed atoms with newly stimulated atoms (gas and liquid lasers).

Once they produce this population inversion (by pumping energy into the laser material), laser scientists trigger the simultaneous decay of all these "excited" atoms by using mirrors, as shown in Figure 5–5. As excited atoms begin to decay, the emitted radiation is reflected back and forth by the mirrors through the laser material. Since these initial emitted and reflected photons are of the right frequency, they in turn stimulate excited atoms along the laser axis to decay, producing more radiation of the same frequency. Moreover, these newly produced photons are in step with the original stimulating photons (i.e., their wave amplitudes match up and add together), amplifying the radiation reflecting back and forth within the laser.[3]

Figure 5–5: Laser beam produced by stimulated emission enhanced by mirrors

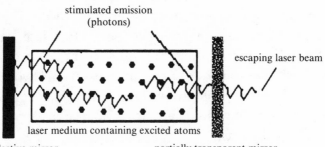

stimulated emission
(photons)

escaping laser beam

laser medium containing excited atoms

100% reflective mirror   partially transparent mirror

One final technological step is required to get the reflecting-oscillating laser beam *out of* the laser material: one of the mirrors is only partly reflective, permitting the internally oscillating and building laser beam to escape in the form of the narrow light beam we see at a laser show or which the grocery clerk uses to read bar codes. Once all the atoms have decayed, the laser pulse ends, and the depleted atoms must be reexcited or replaced by excited atoms.

The process of producing lasers may sound a little racy, but the results have proved a technological boon. Lasers are now an everyday part of our lives: they provide our music by "reading" optical compact discs; they tell the cash register how much we owe; they guide the manufacturing of our computer chips; they cut, drill, and weld metal; they guide our missiles with deadly accuracy; they will serve as futuristic ray guns; they even perform near painless and bloodless surgery on our ailing bodies.

Indeed, lasers have become some of the most powerful devices in our modern, technological society, but they certainly are no proof of the existence of crystal power. The energies lasers transform are very real energies; in fact, lasers are rather inefficient, requiring three to a hundred times as much input energy as they put out. Now, if some crystal worker could "think" a ruby crystal into producing a visible red laser beam, then we might have some physical evidence that crystal-power energies really exist!

Until that time, we have to accept the fact that lasers provide no more support for crystal power than integrated semc on-ductor circuits or crystal radios. In each case, real energy (the kind that costs money) is inputted, and real energy comes out. That old truism still holds: you can't get something for nothing!

Merely thinking "Program, crystal," "Rise, stone," "Give me a car, O great crystal spirit" isn't going to have much impact in the real world.

6

THE PLACEBO EFFECT

W hen *Washington Post* writer Don Oldenburg asked during a phone interview,[1] "Well, isn't this 'crystal power' something like a placebo effect?" it occurred to me that, indeed, the placebo effect could explain much of the reported "successes" in many esoteric fields—acupuncture, homeopathy, faith healing, perhaps even astrology. I had had some scientific training in the use and statistical measurement of placebos in experimental control groups and, as a statistician, I vaguely equated the placebo effect with the Hawthorne effect, a well-known principle found during statistical testing.

The Hawthorne effect is based on the observed fact that people participating in a survey or experiment tend to want to please the researchers, giving answers and responses they think the researchers want to hear and see. Like the placebo effect in medical research, the Hawthorne effect is one of the main reasons social scientists use control groups in their experiments. The Hawthorne effect was first discovered in the 1930s by researchers investigating the effect of increased lighting on productivity at Western Electric's Hawthorne manufacturing plant. First, the researchers observed that workers were indeed more productive under higher levels of illumination, but when the experiment was repeated with a control group whose light conditions the researchers only pretended to increase, much to the scientists' surprise productivity also increased![2]

Obviously, increasing the amount of light alone could not account for the observed improvements; something else had to be going on, and that "something else" has come to be called the Hawthorne effect. I have defined the Hawthorne effect as *the tendency for human experimental subjects to react and/or respond in ways they think will please the researchers.* Normally, we think of this wanting to please as a *voluntary* response—that is, the subjects are voluntarily acting the way they perceive the researchers want them to act. In the case of the original Hawthorne plant study, workers may not have voluntarily, or consciously, increased their work output, but just the fact that they knew they were being paid attention—and being watched—had a positive effect on their level of productivity.

In short, the Hawthorne plant workers may have *subconsciously* worked harder and faster. Thus, there may be four separate components of the Hawthorne effect:

1. Voluntary and conscious pleasing of researchers (subjects deliberately changing their responses and behavior);
2. Voluntary and subconscious pleasing of researchers

(subjects wanting to change their responses and behavior but not consciously aware of how they're doing it);
3. Involuntary and conscious pleasing of researchers (subjects wanting to change, and somehow able to change what are normally involuntary reactions);
4. Involuntary and subconscious pleasing of researchers (subjects not aware of their desire to change to suit researchers' expectations).

In any given group of people and situations, some may respond voluntarily and consciously, while others change their behavior involuntarily and subconsciously; thus, any of the four components may contribute to any observed Hawthorne effect. For scientists, the Hawthorne effect is perceived as rather a nuisance, something that has to be controlled for, necessitating twice as many subjects, doubling the research effort, time, and money. Rarely do researchers investigate the causes and mechanisms of the Hawthorne effect itself.

Likewise, the *placebo effect* is considered a nuisance by most medical researchers, requiring "double-blind" experiments, in which neither the researcher nor the subjects know who's receiving the placebo pill made of an inert substance and visually identical to the real active medicine. Figure 6-1 illustrates the classic double-blind experiment, consisting of an experimental group receiving the real medicine and a control group, which gets a look-alike placebo.

Figure 6-1: Double Blind Experiment

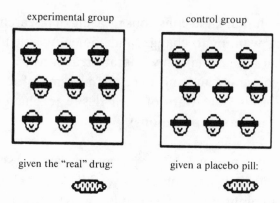

experimental group   control group

given the "real" drug: given a placebo pill:

Neither the researchers nor the subjects know who's getting
the "real" drug and who's getting the placebo pill

Placebos raise an ethical question: How can researchers in all good conscience continue to give a worthless placebo when the real experimental drug has been shown to help relieve patients' suffering? Some years ago, considerable controversy arose when it was discovered that doctors had continued giving prisoners placebo pills for syphilis long after penicillin had been proven to cure the disease. Today, the same controversy swirls around the testing of experimental drugs for AIDS; patients facing a long-suffering death from the fatal disease feel used and abused because neither they nor their doctors know if they are receiving the real drug or a placebo. A recent TV news interview with a female AIDS patient and her doctor showed frustration by both of them; however, as we shall see shortly, the doctor seemed to be making a serious procedural mistake in expressing his own doubts about whether or not the patient was receiving the real drug *because researcher attitude may play a major role in the placebo effect.*

Placebo Effect: The Controversy

As I began research for this book, I realized I needed to learn much more about the placebo effect, so I took advantage of my computer-research capabilities and performed a computer literature search of the medical literature abstracted in Dialog's Knowledge Index™ medical database, MEDI1 (MED-LINE, 1980 to the present), using a simple search strategy: ?FIND PLACEBO EFFECT.

The computer listed 141 articles and papers on the placebo effect, which I reviewed and printed as abstracts. Immediately, I could see that I had hit a goldmine; the placebo effect was indeed becoming a very important and controversial issue in modern medicine. Some of the titles included:

"The Placebo Effect: Real or Imaginary?"
"Homeopathy: Merely a Placebo Effect?"
"The Placebo Effect: A Controversy"
"Suggestibility and Placebo Effect" (editorial)
"Truth Telling, Placebos, and Deception: Ethical and
    Legal Issues in Practice"

"Physician Beliefs, Attitudes, and Prescribing Behavior
 for Anti-inflamatory Drugs"
"Understanding Placebos in Dentistry"
"How Much of the Placebo 'Effect' Is Really Statistical
 Regression?"
"In Search of a Status for Acupuncture"
"The Placebo Effect Reconsidered"
"Biofeedback and the Placebo Effect"
"Magnetic Necklace: Its Therapeutic Effectiveness on
 Neck and Shoulder Pain."

Not only did the titles suggest considerable controversy building up about the placebo effect but the articles came from
a wide variety of medical fields: dentistry, geriatric nursing,
psychiatry, surgery, family medicine, allergy and immunology,
sociology, rheumatology, space science, biofeedback. They
were also from a wide variety of countries: Britain, Canada,
Spain, France, Portugal, Belgium, South Africa, and the
United States. How many of these authors were aware of
the work on placebos being done in other fields and countries?
Could it be that the international medical community was
approaching a watershed or major breakthrough in understanding how the placebo effect works?

Perhaps the most surprising claim regarding the placebo
effect is that, prior to the age of modern medicine, almost
all medical successes could be attributed to the placebo effect.
One oft-quoted expert on the placebo effect writes, "Since
almost all medications until recently were placebos, the history

of medical treatment can be characterized largely as the history of the placebo effect."[3]

Is this pure arrogance on the part of a highly successful doctor, or was early medicine really a hit or miss situation? Certainly, it has been proven that some traditional herbal remedies have active pharmacological agents (e.g., willow bark was a precursor to aspirin), but how many of these were discovered and/or applied correctly? Certainly, too, many early medical practices were actually harmful to the patients—most notably, blood-letting—and many prescribed medicines were actually toxic.

Suggestibility and faith have long been associated with the placebo effect: the patient must be suggestible and have faith that the physician's curative methods really work. As early as the sixteenth century, Montaigne wrote about the power of suggestibility:

> I am one of those who are most sensible of the power of imagination: everyone is jostled by it, but some are overthrown by it. . . . Why do the physicians possess, beforehand, their patients' credulity with so many false promises of cure, if not to the end, that the effect of imagination may supply the imposture of their decoctions. They know very well that a great master of their trade has given it under his hand, that he has known some with whom the very sight of physic would work.[4]

By the seventeenth and eighteenth centuries, physicians and writers generally recognized suggestion—the power of positive expectation—as a significant part of medical practice. The word *placebo* comes from the Latin verb of the same spelling, meaning "I shall please." Placebo became an official medical term in the late 1700s, defined as "a commonplace method or medicine" in the *New Medical Dictionary* by Motherby.[5] Even Thomas Jefferson wrote, "One of the most successful physicians I have ever known, has assured me that he used more of bread pills, drops of colored water, and powders of hickory ashes, than of all other medicines put together."[6]

Modern doctors suggest, perhaps a bit arrogantly: "Prior to the advent of scientific medicine near the turn of the twentieth century, most remedies administered by physicians had little or no curative power in themselves. . . ."[7]

Yet, patients *were* cured, *did* get well, in spite of their physicians' placebo prescriptions. Somehow, physicians, healers, and shamans throughout the ages and in all cultures managed to cure a significant portion of their patients. How? Is the placebo effect so widespread and powerful that doctors throughout the ages have built their reputations on it?

The answer is yes, but how they did so is not easily answered. Modern studies of the placebo effect show that it is effective 30% to 50% of the time, with one study showing that placebos are 60% as effective as real painkillers: aspirin and morphine. The placebo effect is surprisingly constant and effective for a wide variety of diseases and medical conditions, ranging from arthritis to headaches, from back problems to heart trouble. Placebos are even effective in reducing or eliminating pain during surgery.

In a review of the medical literature, Dr. H. K. Beecher found that an average of 35.2% of 1,082 total patients benefited from placebos.[8] Specific diseases in which the placebo effect has been found to work include angina pectoris, rheumatoid and degenerative arthritis, pain, hayfever, headache, cough, peptic ulcer, hypertension, and especially anxiety and depression.[9]

Think about that. Here is a medical "treatment" that helps cure 35% of all sufferers of a wide variety of ailments and which has been given credit for almost all medical "cures" throughout history. In short, the placebo effect must be the single most effective medicine known to man. However, doctors not only don't make use of it but they talk of placebos in derogatory tones!

The Universal Medicine

The placebo effect, then, must be considered the "universal cure" so long sought and claimed by so many quacks. Oddly enough, a placebo can be anything, any form of treatment. We normally think of placebos as medically inactive pills: sugar pills, bread pills—any inert, tasteless substance in pill or capsule form. However, any treatment may be considered a placebo. Surprisingly, placebo surgeries have been performed; a group of angina patients underwent a mock procedure in which the chest was cut but the artery was not touched. These patients showed the same improvement in heart function as angina surgery patients.[10]

In the case of psychotherapy, the distinction between a "real" treatment and a placebo treatment is harder to make. Is Freudian therapy any less of a placebo than Jungian therapy —or even Scientology, for that matter? All brands of psychotherapy direct attention toward the patient; suddenly, someone *cares,* someone is paying attention. That caring, that attention, may be the real therapy, not analyzing whether you hate your mother or if your id is in conflict with your superego.

For instance, one study found that 80% of schizophrenic patients improved because they were receiving greater attention—in spite of the fact that the attention they received was not intended to be therapeutic![11]

Similarly, a series of studies were made on hospitalized depressed patients who would normally receive drug-therapy treatment. One group of forty-four depressed patients received only a placebo, but they were otherwise treated the same as patients receiving active drugs; 50% of the placebo patients showed high improvement in their mental illness. More importantly, both patient and physician attitudes were shown to affect how much the depressed patients improved: "favorable patient attitudes toward the use of chemotherapy bore a strong relationship with the outcome."[12]

In short, mentally ill patients who believe the medication will work are much more likely to get better. To a lesser extent, patients whose doctors also believe in the value of the treatment are more likely to improve.

Similar studies of physically ill patients have also tried to link patient and doctor attitudes with the placebo response, with mixed results. But, especially for patients experiencing pain and trying to get relief, placebos work best for patients *expecting* the medication to relieve pain. Oddly enough, those patients experiencing high levels of pain are more likely to get relief from a placebo than those experiencing minor pain. Even odder yet, those patients who receive *higher doses* of the placebo get greater relief![13]

In short, patients who *expect* the medication or treatment to work are more likely to show a positive response to placebos than those who have doubts. *Suggestion* also plays a role; patients whose doctors display a positive attitude toward the value of the treatment are more likely to get better than those whose doctors express doubt. Thus, the unfortunate AIDS patient whose doctor expressed doubt about whether or not she was receiving real medication or a placebo was actually being cheated by her doctor, because the placebo effect does not disappear simply because the medication is real. Most experts now agree that the placebo effect plays an important role in active, real medications and that a doctor who expresses doubt or a negative attitude toward the treatment may well cause the patient not to respond normally to the drug.

Dr. Beecher points out, "Not only do placebos produce beneficial results, but like other therapeutic agents they have associated toxic effects." Among the undesirable side effects of placebos are dry mouth, nausea, sensation of heaviness, headache, difficulty concentrating, drowsiness, warm glow, relaxation, fatigue, sleep, weakness, palpitation, rash, and diarrhea.[14]

If the placebo effect can have such a wide range of both

desirable and undesirable results, it must indeed be the most powerful universal medicine known to man!

Theories and Explanations

Despite all the studies, experiments, and statistics, modern medicine still does not fully understand how the placebo effect works. The literature reveals as many theories as authors. Some experts focus on the power of suggestion, others on faith, belief, and expectation. Others tie suggestibility to the ability to be hypnotized (while admittedly finding little statistical correlation), while others focus on patients' psychological states. Biofeedback experts point to their success in relieving pain and influencing involuntary functions as a possible mechanism for the placebo effect, while psychologists cite esoteric theories of "transitional phenomena" and "control theory." Finally, some recent studies suggest that the body's own natural pain relievers—endorphins, which are morphine-like substances—play a role in the placebo response.[15]

At least two authors have linked the placebo effect to the Hawthorne effect, much as I did when I first began studying the placebo effect: "This phenomenon is similar to what has become known in industry as the 'Hawthorne effect' whereby the efficiency of factory workers was found to improve as a direct result of the increased attention received during investigation."[16]

Hard-core skeptics relegate the placebo response to

spontaneous remission, the fact that almost any disease can suddenly reverse itself and the patient get well for no discernible reason.

Yet, for all their theories, the experts admit that they have had little success in predicting which patients will show a positive reaction to placebos. Indeed, some patients who show no positive placebo response in one test will later react positively in another test. To a scientific mind, this is all very confusing; medicines are supposed to work in a rather straight-forward cause-and-effect fashion: a patient takes a drug and subsequently gets better. How can a treatment be effective part of the time with some patients and then reverse itself to prove ineffective, while curing other patients who were previously unaffected by the placebo?

How, indeed? The placebo effect would seem to be as mysterious and confusing as medicine itself to the average layman. Perhaps Sudhir Kakar, in his classic study of Indian shamans and mystics, stated it best when describing how an Indian peasant chose his particular healer:

> "It is the *vishwas* a healer inspires which is crucial," he [the peasant] had said, using a Hindi word that denotes both trust and confidence. And how did a healer inspire the *vishwas?* From his groping attempts at putting into words what is clearly a matter of feeling, he conveyed that whereas one level of a patient's interaction with the healer is the talk about symptoms, their etiology, the possible therapy and the prognosis, there is another and perhaps more significant exchange taking place simultaneously. In this other conversation carried out without words and below the threshold of consciousness, the patient

is busy registering whether and how well the doctor opposite him fits into his culturally determined image of the ideal healer. . . . It was also obvious that not only the healer but the healing process too is located at the edge of the society, in the sense that religious restrictions and social taboos tend to be suspended for the duration of the healing encounter.[17]

In short, if a patient believes that a doctor or healer is right for him, fits his preconceived notion of what a healer should be, then the patient is far more likely to get better, *even if the therapy is contrary to his normal social behavior,* as for example, taking drugs, talking about normally taboo subjects, changing his diet, allowing needles and knives to cut into his flesh, screaming at the top of his lungs, praying to obscure gods, or holding a crystal against his forehead.

Crystal Power and the Placebo Effect

What does all this mean to us and our study of crystal power? Hopefully, a lot of things:

1. When looking at medical claims for crystal power, we must assume the placebo effect will yield at least a 35% cure rate in reducing pain and improving many disease conditions.
2. For psychological claims of self-improvement, we can expect the placebo and/or Hawthorne effect to result in a 50% to 80% cure rate.

3. Likewise, we must assume the placebo effect also operates in all other esoteric types of "medical" treatments—acupuncture, magnetic necklaces, faith healing, shamanism, voodoo, witchcraft, color analysis, etc.
4. In light of all the medical evidence for the placebo effect, we must recognize the power of the mind and/or subconscious in controlling and affecting our bodies' health and well-being.
5. Perhaps most importantly, we must recognize how powerful the placebo effect is and urge further research to understand how it operates and how we can learn to take advantage of it.

As we shall see in Chapter 9, 38% of surveyed crystal workers claim to use crystal power for healing others. Note how close that 38% figure is to the expected placebo response rate of 35%. Likewise, the survey found that 56% of crystal workers claim to use crystals for self-healing, while 59% use crystals for meditation and/or self-improvement. Again, note that these 56% and 59% figures are within the 50% to 80% range expected for placebo response in psychological treatments.

While no experimental research has been done on the medical claims for crystal power, British researchers have compared acupuncture with a placebo treatment (sham transcutaneous nerve stimulation) and found no statistically significant difference between the two. The researchers concluded, "Although the results favoured acupuncture, this may be because acupuncture offered more suggestion than the placebo and thus had a greater placebo effect."[18]

The movie, *Leap of Faith,* offers a good study of how acupuncture can serve as a very powerful suggestive treatment: the heroine is battling terminal lymphatic cancer and just holding her own with the help of a clinical pyschologist, who believes in the power of the mind to overcome physical diseases. Then the heroine visits an acupuncturist who lives in a woodland setting, which is exotic, peaceful, and suggestive. Obviously, the acupuncture setting, with its mystical oriental overtones, is exactly what the heroine has been looking for; as Sudhir Kakar would say, the acupuncturist fit her "culturally determined image of the ideal healer," and, of course, the heroine is cured of her cancer—much to the astonishment of her regular medical doctor.

Are such miracles possible? Can belief, faith, expectation, and suggestion really produce miracle cures? Perhaps overcoming terminal cancer is a bit too much to expect, but the power of the placebo effect can indeed bring about minor miracles for at least a third of all sufferers of a wide variety of ailments. Can we fault patients—unhappy with a business-like Western medical treatment—for trying esoteric treatments like acupuncture, crystal power, and faith healing, which offer a more suggestive, placebo-inducing environment? Perhaps the Western medical profession can learn from these methods and strive to provide a more supportive, placebo-inducing setting. If modern medicine could add the power of the placebo effect to its growing list of active medicines and treatments, then the patient could have the best of both worlds and would not have to resort to treatments by untrained personnel, who promise everything and deliver only placebos—which often are harmful because they delay needed, proven treatments.

7

THE POWER
OF THE MIND:
YOGA, BIOFEEDBACK,
HYPNOSIS, AND
FAITH HEALING

Like many of my fellow skeptics in CSICOP and the Bay Area Skeptics, I have long had an interest in the esoteric. After all, that's how most of us became involved in the field in the first place. It is easy for scientists to reject out of hand anything that smacks of mysticism and unscientific claims. It's much harder, however, to put aside one's scientific prejudice long enough to study and try to understand what the esoteric "arts" are all about. At every turn, the scientist runs into claims that go against everything he has learned is possible: levitation, reincarnation, thought transference, astral projection, spirit entities, "space brothers," *chakras,* gods, and ascended masters.

Small wonder that the average scientist recoils in horror, utters some disdainful comments, and retreats to the intellectual safety of his chosen field. Studying the esoteric is not for the narrow-minded, the faint of heart, or—contrary to popular scientific opinion—the weak-minded. For one thing, there's a whole new language to learn, much of it foreign, plus mind-boggling concepts not even hinted at in traditional Western education. To the Western mind, most of the Eastern esoteric traditions seem silly and not worth studying. Yet, it must be remembered that over three-quarters of the world's population has long been steeped in such esoteric traditions, that Western civilization and its emphasis on the material world are relative newcomers to human thought.

Prehistoric shamanism, Eastern mysticism, and folkloric superstition held sway for thousands of years, providing people with their only source of medicine, psychology, and spiritual refuge. As the modern New Age adherents would say, "There must be something to it."

I suggest that that "something" might well be the placebo effect, plus its counterpart in the psychological realm, the Hawthorne effect.

As we noted in Chapter 6, modern science does not understand the mechanism or mechanisms behind the placebo effect, although terms like *expectation, suggestion,* and *suggestibility* are offered as explanations. Whatever the actual mechanism, the placebo effect offers proof and demonstration that the power of the mind is greater than we, in Western science, think, but is probably less powerful than New Age proponents and Eastern mystics claim. Some middle ground is probably closer to the truth; and, as the modern literature on the placebo effect indicates, some medical researchers and doctors are beginning to realize that placebos may be more important than their use as mere controls in double-blind experiments.

A radio talk-show host, Dr. Dean Edell, often mentions the placebo effect as evidence of the power of the mind. "If believing in a placebo, a sugar pill, can cure us, why not eliminate the middle man and just believe in ourselves—believe in our power to heal ourselves?"[1]

Unfortunately, the placebo effect may not be that simple; cultural upbringing, current state of mind, healer-patient interaction—all seem to play a role. We're probably a long way from being able to will ourselves to be well, but at least two fields of study—one ancient, one modern—claim to be able to do just that: teach us how to control involuntary bodily functions and thus give us the ability to produce our own state of health. Yoga, the ancient oriental discipline, teaches both physical and mental exercises that give the yogi surprising control over his body and mind. Biofeedback, the modern science of detecting, measuring, and displaying brain and body activity, can also teach us similar control over involuntary functions—without the years or decades of study required to master yoga.

Yoga, Biofeedback, and Crystal Power

The yogi adept can slow his heartbeat to a crawl, bring his breathing to a virtual stop, and go into alpha-wave trance states for long periods of time. Biofeedback subjects—connected to elaborate equipment that detect and display brain waves, electrical activity on the skin, muscle tension, or the like—likewise can learn to control heart rate, galvanic skin response, blood pressure, and a host of other involuntary functions long thought to be beyond man's voluntary control. Thus both the yogi and the biofeedback subject can learn to control the state of their minds and bodies to reduce medical complications—relieve anxiety and tension, raise or lower blood pressure, get rid of headaches, and lessen pain.

Figure 7–1 shows a simple biofeedback setup to measure muscle tension by measuring the tiny voltages (around 50 millionths of a volt) produced by the muscle cells as they contract and recover. In this case, electrodes on the forehead pick up the tiny AC voltages from the frontalis muscle (a major source of tension headaches); a series of amplifiers, electrical filters, and rectifiers turn the tiny muscle-voltage signal into an audio tone that is fed back to the subject through earphones. (The signal may also be displayed on a meter or digital readout.) The louder the tone, the greater the muscle tension. Thus, the biofeedback subject who suffers from tension headaches can learn to will the audio tone lower and lower in volume, at the same time reducing the muscle voltage and tension that is causing his headaches. In one study, five tension headache patients were able to reduce the intensity of their headaches by a factor of three over a five-week period of biofeedback training.[2]

Figure 7–1: Biofeedback Setup to Reduce Headaches from Muscle Tension

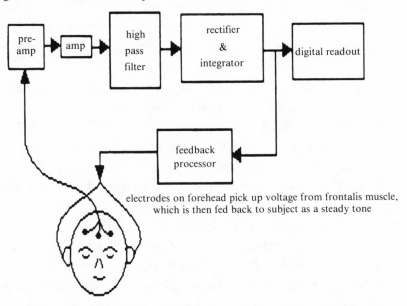

electrodes on forehead pick up voltage from frontalis muscle, which is then fed back to subject as a steady tone

Yoga, on the other hand, requires years of training, not weeks. Classical yoga consists of two major disciplines: *hatha*-yoga (physical) and *raja*-yoga (mental). Hatha-yoga teaches a graduated series of stretching and breathing exercises—done quietly, slowly and with a minimum of movement—that involve nearly every muscle in the body. I have studied and practiced hatha-yoga off and on for many years, and I can personally attest to the physical benefits of such a regimen; probably no other set of exercises provides better muscle tension-opposition toning for the amount of effort expended. Hatha-yoga also teaches proper breathing through full use of the diaphragm. Once the yoga novice has mastered at least some hatha-yoga, he or she then proceeds to the mental exercises of raja-yoga, usually of two types: visualization (for instance, focusing on a candle, then maintaining that image with eyes closed) and what's called stilling the mind (stemming the flow of thoughts). In modern biofeedback terminology, this corresponds to entering the relaxed alpha state, wherein the midfrequency alpha brain-waves dominate.

For me, and I suspect for many Westerners, raja-yoga is a near impossibility, particularly stemming the flow of thoughts that occupy our minds throughout much of the day and night. This characteristic, the constant flow of thought, varies from individual to individual; some people seem to be relatively free of such preoccupation, while others are hardly able to turn off the flow. In many respects, this division of mental processes reminds me very much of the modern categorization of left-brained and right-brained people. Science has discovered that the left side of the brain controls linear thought processes such as language, logic, and mathematics, while the right side of the brain is associated with nonlinear thought processes such as intuition and visualization. My colleague Dr. Mort Litwack, author of *The Art of Self-Fulfillment,* often tells me, "You're an extremely left-brain thinker; you need to balance that with some nonlinear right-brain activity."

Perhaps that's why I also have tremendous trouble with

visualization; the candle-flame image only lasts for a few moments at most. Obviously, some people can visualize much quicker, more easily, and more vividly than others—and that imaging ability may prove very important to our study of crystal power. Chapters 2 and 3 described many claims for crystal power which involved visualization: picturing a crystal becoming clearer, visualizing the crystal growing to the size of a house, visually focusing on crystal balls until an image appears, using a crystal to remember dreams, picturing the car you want.

New Age crystal power depends heavily on this ability to visualize; those who are able to visualize easily are more likely to be attracted to crystal "work" because they are able to do the mental exercises suggested, and perhaps the crystal visions provide an outlet, a unique means of using their native ability. Such visualization may even help resolve some right-brain conflicts or enhance right-brain intuitive processes.

However, there is one major difference between the claims for raja-yoga and the claims for crystal power: yoga only claims to enhance the power to control one's *own* mind and body, while crystal-power advocates claim to be able to influence not only their own minds and bodies but also the minds and bodies of others, as well as to influence external events. To the yoga purist, such claims are anathema, reeking of power, greed, and other-worldliness. Yoga adepts do hint at greater powers, such as levitation, spirit contact, and ESP, but these are considered the dark side of yoga—to be renounced and avoided in order to attain purity of thought and perfect detachment from the physical world.

Personally, I've given up trying to achieve stillness of mind and perfect detachment—not that I was sure I wanted to achieve such a state in the first place! As a writer, I find the constant flow of thoughts very useful; I can compose entire articles or sections of books in my head, say in 30 minutes to an hour, prior to touching finger to keyboard. Short pieces, such as letters to the editor, will often come out in a word-for-word transcript of my mental version, while longer versions tend to be shaped and reshaped by the words as they appear on screen or paper, leading to mental continuations until the original mental concept has been fulfilled. Thus, I can have a mental image of a piece of writing—down to the exact wording if I can only recall it—yet no visual image at all.

Oddly enough, my dreams are quite visual and colorful, and I can recall long segments at will without placing a crystal under my pillow. Dream experts now teach patients how to remember their dreams, and even how to remain consciously aware while dreaming. Crystal-power advocates, then, who claim to program crystals like a VCR to record and play back dreams, are most likely only programming themselves to remember that night's dream; they use the crystal as a programmed reminder—much like a posthypnotic suggestion.

Hypnosis, because it depends on suggestion and the subject's suggestibility, is often mentioned in conjunction with the placebo effect. Indeed, for that rare 15% of the population who is able to be deeply hypnotized, hypnosis is far more powerful and effective than placebos for reducing pain. Yet studies have found "no correlation between response to placebo and hypnotic responsivity."[3]

Like yoga, hypnosis induces a trance, instantly placing the subject into a deep alpha state; it could easily be argued that yogis are practicing self-hypnosis in achieving their states

Figure 7 2: Four Main Types of Brain Rhythms (EEG)

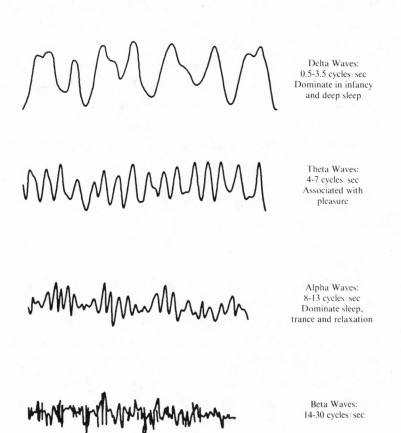

Delta Waves:
0.5-3.5 cycles/sec
Dominate in infancy
and deep sleep

Theta Waves:
4-7 cycles/sec
Associated with
pleasure

Alpha Waves:
8-13 cycles/sec
Dominate sleep,
trance and relaxation

Beta Waves:
14-30 cycles/sec

of relaxation. Again, like yoga, hypnosis can also be used to control involuntary functions: relieving pain, slowing the heart rate, or reducing the craving for nicotine, for example.

The common denominator in all of this—yoga, biofeedback, hypnosis—is the alpha state, the term used by biofeedback experts to indicate when brain-wave patterns become dominated by the midfrequency alpha waves (8 to 13 cycles per second). Figure 7–2 illustrates the four recognized types of brain waves as measured by an EEG (electroencephalogram). The slowest delta waves dominate during the first year of life, then usually appear only during deep sleep or localized in association with brain disease. Alpha waves are the most prominent of adult brain waves, are nearly always present, and become dominant during certain stages of sleep, trance, and deep relaxation. Alpha waves have the same frequency as our period of visual persistence (10 per second) and have been associated by some experts with the brain's scanning process. Theta waves have been associated with pleasure, since pleasant mental images are evoked when theta waves dominate.[4]

Alpha training, using relaxation and visualization techniques, has reached almost cultic proportions. I've met some quite down-to-earth people who raved about alpha training, particularly the ability to achieve intuitive right-brain visualization on the "screen of the mind." This alpha visualization sounds suspiciously similar to crystal-power visualization, even to the claim to be able to influence external events and heal others at a distance.[5]

Since the basic structure of the human mind has not changed in thousands, if not millions, of years, it seems reasonable to assume that such alpha visualization may have been involved in many of the esoteric practices we've discussed and some we haven't: shamanism, crystal-ball and water scrying, crystal spirits, channeling, yoga, levitation, astral projection, Edgar Cayce's faith healing—to name a few. For some reason, visualizing while in the alpha trance state of deep relaxation makes the visions more real, more connected, making it seem that they take on a life of their own. Small wonder the ancient shamans, mystics, and crystal gazers thought they were onto something big; they had entered a new mental state where the power of the mind somehow seemed to control and manipulate the real world!

Isn't that what crystal power is really all about: trying to increase the power of the mind to control and manipulate the external world?

As we've seen, the mind *can* control and change *some* things, most notably one's own mind, body, and state of well-being. Beyond that, I'm afraid, alpha-power and crystal-power advocates alike are treading on weak or dangerous ground, heading for self-delusion and perhaps even mental illness. Consider all the channelers around today, thousands of otherwise sane people who believe that they talk to dead spirits, "ascended masters," "space brothers," Atlanteans, gods—you name it. Not so long ago, such unfortunate people who heard voices and talked to gods were institutionalized; now they write books, give seminars, and make lots of money. Are they deluded? Frankly, I hope so! The real world is complex enough without an invisible entourage of spirits and "space brothers" to worry about!

Faith Healing

So far, we have only mentioned faith healing in passing, yet there is an obvious connection between the medical claims for crystal power and the claims for faith healing. Many of the same elements are present in both: belief in an esoteric healing system, suggestibility and expectation on the part of believers, suggestion on the part of the "healer," often accompanied by trance states. But finally, of course, the placebo effect must be assumed to operate in *all* medical and psychological healing situations.

While faith healing normally lies in the purview of my colleagues James Randi and Dr. Wallace Sampson, I will venture a few personal observations here since I participated in the somewhat famous investigation of Peter Popoff's faith-healing session held in San Francisco in 1986. While James Randi and the Bay Area Skeptics were recording Mrs. Popoff sending secret radio messages to a tiny microphone allegedly hidden in Peter Popoff's ear—names, addresses, diseases—I was busy conversing by sign language with a young deaf man who had been following Popoff around northern California for weeks, spending rent money on transportation and donating the suggested $100 per performance, all in the hope that Popoff would call him up to the stage and "pop" him on the forehead.

In fact, as I slowly learned via sign language, the young man had already been "popped" a couple of weeks before at the Sacramento "healings"—popped so hard that his ears rang! But the "cure" hadn't taken, and he was back in San Francisco asking only two things: to be able to hear and to have enough money to live on—while another $50 went into the envelope.

Unfortunately, no amount of faith, crystal-power, hypnosis, placebos, or alpha training can cure the physically deaf—nor the two blind men Rev. Popoff passed by without taking the opportunity to "heal." Suggestion, faith, the Hawthorne effect, the placebo effect only extend so far, can help only in certain ailments: pain, and conditions controllable by the human mind.

On the other hand, a 35% success rate for placebos is not bad; a 50% to 80% success rate for the psychological Hawthorne effect is nothing to sneeze at either. Add to those rates biofeedback and relaxation training, and it is possible to envision a whole host of medical ailments treated and relieved by mind power alone—if only the medical profession could figure out how best to put such techniques into practice. Use of placebos—whether sugar pills or sham psychotherapy—raises serious ethical questions, while developing the requisite healer-patient attitudes and relationships would require serious retraining for most doctors.

The best solution would be to understand fully this complex mind-body interface that involves faith, suggestion, expectation, alpha waves, trance states, and visualization. Normally, once science understands how a process works, it can replicate that process through control variables (for instance, by evoking the proper psychological state of expectancy to be healed). I suppose the danger might be that, by scientifically removing the mystery, the power of the placebo could disappear as well.

8

CRYSTAL POWER AND PARAPSYCHOLOGY

Many of the claims for crystal power involve ESP (extrasensory perception), telekinesis (moving physical objects by the mind alone), precognition (predicting the future), and other alleged human abilities normally investigated within the field of parapsychology. The basic underlying claim is that crystals somehow enhance, amplify, and transmit parapsychological forces and energies (bioplasmic or orgone energy) generated by humans. Crystals, the advocates claim, vibrate in response to this mysterious energy and—just as vibrating crystals pick up and amplify radio waves—amplify and retransmit stronger parapsychological energies.

In theory, then, the use of crystals should greatly improve the performance of subjects in parapsychological experiments. Although I haven't heard of any such experiments yet, the beneficial effect of crystals should immediately be picked up dramatically by the experimenters' statistical analysis—any small improvement in subjects' performance would be reported as beating incredible odds against chance, 100,000–to–1 or 1–million–to–1 odds.

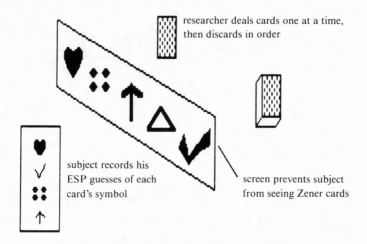

researcher deals cards one at a time, then discards in order

subject records his ESP guesses of each card's symbol

screen prevents subject from seeing Zener cards

Figure 8–1: Zener Card Experiment

To see how statistics works in ESP testing, consider the basic Zener card experiment, pictured in Figure 8–1. The deck of twenty-five cards consists of five symbols, so there are five cards of each symbol. The experimenter shuffles the cards, then draws the top card and looks at it behind the screen out of view of the subject, who then guesses the card's symbol and records the guess; the experimenter discards the first card and looks at the next symbol. Random chance should yield one in five successes; with a deck of twenty-five cards, the average person with no ESP ability should guess five of the twenty-five cards correctly by pure chance. If the deck is reshuffled and the experiment repeated four times, for a total of one hundred cards and guesses, random chance would yield twenty correct guesses.

Now, statistics tells us (see Table 8–1) that if the ESP subject correctly guesses twenty-eight of the one hundred cards (eight more than pure chance), the experiment becomes statistically significant at the .05 level (20–to–1 odds). If the subject guesses thirty-two of the one hundred cards correctly, the statistical odds go up to 325–to–1. Now, suppose the ESP subject uses a crystal to "greatly improve" his or her ESP power, for example, doubling the random chance rate of twenty to forty correct card guesses (still only a 40% success rate). Statistics would evaluate the significance of the "crystal-enhanced" ESP subject as 1,744,272–to–1 odds against chance.

If the crystal-using ESP subject were to continue at the same level of performance, doubling the chance rate for 250 cards (guessing 100 correctly, compared to the chance rate of 50), statisticians would now declare the results incredibly significant, around 375 trillion–to–1 odds against chance!

Today, parapsychologists are happy to report any results with statistically significant odds more than twenty to one, so any experiments with results as statistically significant as 100,000–to–1 would create intense interest and scrutiny.

TABLE 8–1
How Statisticians Evaluate ESP Experimental Odds[1]

100 Trials (Cards)		250 Trials (Cards)	
Correct Guesses	Odds	Correct Guesses	Odds
20	random	50	random
24	3 to 1	56	3 to 1
28	20 to 1	63	20 to 1
32	325 to 1	69	330 to 1
36	15,782 to 1	75	12,943 to 1
40	1,744,272 to 1	82	2,380,721 to 1
		88	533,483,935 to 1
		94	287.7 billion to 1
		100	375.3 trillion to 1

Note: These figures have been calculated by a computer program using a double-precision power series approximation to the normal probability integral.

Although crystal-power advocates have been claiming for several years that crystals increase their ESP power, no triumphant experimental evidence has been produced. Either the experiments have not been done (in which case the para-psychologists are missing a great opportunity, since major claims to increase ESP power don't come along every day), or the results have been disappointing and hence have gone unreported.

ESP and the Power of the Mind

Let's put aside for the moment the question of whether or not crystals can amplify and enhance ESP, and look at what ESP is—or is alleged to be—and how the brain can have this mysterious power to read other people's minds, transmit thoughts, or influence external events. We saw in Chapter 7 that the brain does indeed generate electrical brain-wave patterns. Could these be the source of extrasensory perception?

The physicist and electrical engineer would say "highly unlikely" for a number of reasons:

- Brain-wave voltages are extremely tiny, 5 to 50 microvolts (millionths of a volt).
- Brain-wave frequencies range from .5 to 30 cycles per second, with corresponding wavelengths of about 10,000 kilometers, which is far from the radio-frequency range (1,000 to 10 billion cycles per second).
- Since scalp electrodes can detect internal brain-wave voltage differences, the skin must act as a ground for electromagnetic brain waves.
- The most sensitive electomagnetic antenna would be unable to detect brain wave patterns even a few inches away, much less several feet or miles.

In short, so far as the scientist is concerned, brain waves are weak, detectable, but largely confined to the head containing the brain being measured. At least theoretically, electromagnetic-energy transmission between brains is not a likely explanation for ESP. Electrical fields do not extend very far from their sources; for instance, only the highest-voltage power lines (20,000 to 100,000 volts) are suspected of potential harm to people in the immediate vicinity. Brain-wave voltages are a billion times smaller, well beyond normal, long-distance detection range.

However, one scientist, Russian professor I. M. Kogan, has presented scientific calculations that show that electromagnetic radio waves can indeed account for ESP and other parapsychological powers.[2] Kogan calculates that "observed frequencies of brain biocurrents" correspond to radio wavelengths of three hundred kilometers, which would correspond to brain-wave frequencies of a million cycles per second, compared to the highest observed frequencies of thirty cycles per second. Did Professor Kogan make a mistake? Perhaps Kogan was referring to the tiniest squiggles on the EEG machine, which by the greatest stretch of the imagination might reach thousands or perhaps even millions of cycles per second.

But Professor Kogan fails to calculate the projected *power* of the radio waves thus transmitted by the human brain. A commercial radio-broadcasting station consumes 5,000 to 50,000 watts of power to transmit via an extremely efficient antenna to specially designed radio receivers within a hundred daytime miles. The human brain generates perhaps one-billionth of a watt; any radio waves generated would have to be at least five thousand billion times weaker than normal radio waves (occasionally detectable by humans via silver fillings in their teeth).

If we are only occasionally able to detect normal radio waves with the help of a dentist, how can we possibly detect Professor Kogan's "brain radio waves," which must be billions of times weaker?

In *theory*—if not in accuracy of calculations—Professor Kogan is right; *all* alternating electrical currents (including brain waves) generate corresponding radio waves (which are really just a "spreading out into space" of the original electromagnetic field). But has the human animal developed the ability to detect such incredibly weak radio waves? If some special transmitting and receiving glands have evolved, medical science has failed to find them, and such brain-wave-receiving glands would have to be so incredibly sensitive that our electrical lights and power (operating at just double our highest brain-wave frequencies of 30 cycles per second) would totally swamp any possible "brain radio waves."

Now, let's try to apply Professor Kogan's theory of "brain radio waves" to the idea that crystals vibrate in response with such waves, then amplify and retransmit, thus increasing ESP. As we saw in Chapter 5, radio crystals vibrate at from 4.7 million cycles per second to 40 million cycles per second, far above normal brain-wave frequencies of .3 to 30 cycles per second, but close to Kogan's calculated frequencies of a million cycles per second.

Is Professor Kogan right? Does the brain really generate radio waves in the frequency range of a million cycles per second, radio waves that can be picked up and amplified by crystals? Frankly, I doubt it, based on the electrical-power calculations alone, but at least Kogan's theory about ESP has the advantage that it can be scientifically tested: merely construct a radio generator of the proper frequency and see if it can be detected by ESP subjects, or somehow interferes with their ESP ability.

ESP and the Laws of Nature

One of the major reasons I have always felt that ESP—and especially precognition—cannot exist in the real world is that it would violate the laws of nature. We cannot know the future because we could then take steps to change or influence the outcome. (Who would not buy a Lotto ticket if he or she knew the six winning numbers in advance?) So, on the face of it, precognition is out, being a logical impossibility. Thought transference is another matter; after all, we can already transfer thoughts by speaking, writing, body language, sign language, telephone, fax machines, computers, and photographs.

Why would we think another—otherworldly—means of communication is necessary or possible? Obviously, if we think someone is lying to us, and we'd like to know what they are *really* thinking, it might be nice to be able to read their minds. But think what that would do to our social structure! We'd always know what politicians are thinking while delivering their less-than-candid speeches. Jimmy Swaggart's and Jim Bakker's audiences would have known what was *really* on their minds. Mrs. Popoff would not have to use secret radio transmissions to tell Peter names, addresses, and diseases.

Worst of all, if we could read other people's minds, we would always know what they are *really* thinking about us— and how many of us could take that? How long would society survive under such "open-mind" conditions? I suggest, not long!

Of course, parapsychologists retort by saying only *some* people have ESP *some* of the time, bolstering this claim with statistical experiments that might measure some slight ESP ability. I maintain that if ESP ability is so slight that it has to be measured by statistical testing over a long series of experiments and that if not even the ESP subject can tell when a particular guess is accurate, then such an ephemeral psychic ability is not worth a plugged nickle.

Let me give an example or two. Before the Challenger shuttle blew up, not a single psychic predicted the disaster. Yet the disaster was easily predictable, given the freakishly cold weather that day in Florida. Like most Americans that morning, I watched the prelaunch countdown; when I heard that the temperature was down below freezing in the 20s, and forecasters expected it to stay that cold, I said to myself, "They'll never launch today!"

I turned off the TV and went back to work. Later that morning, I drove to the bank; as I approached the automatic teller, a stunned woman came up mumbling, "The shuttle just blew up. The shuttle just blew up."

I couldn't believe my ears. "You mean it blew up on the pad?"

"No, it blew up during launch."

"You're kidding me. They tried to launch in that weather? That's absolutely insane."

The reason that I considered the launch impossible that day was simple: as an engineer, I knew that the operating range for launch temperature began at least 25 degrees above Cape Canaveral's freezing temperatures that day. No engineer in his right mind would turn on such a complex system as the shuttle, knowing operating conditions were well out of the norm. In a sense, I predicted the Challenger disaster at the moment I turned off the TV; I didn't have a flash visualizing a disaster, but I did know from an engineering standpoint that a successful launch was not possible. I'm glad I didn't accidentally turn the TV back on and witness that tragic explosion—how strange I would have felt, having said earlier that the launch couldn't go off!

Was that ESP? No, that was common sense, knowing a little more about the situation than the average viewer. Yet, the feeling I got when told of the disaster must be very similar to the feeling an ESP subject gets when told he's had a successful experimental run—that somehow you beat the odds and "knew" beforehand the results of the experiment. (Certainly, launching the Challenger under those conditions was the biggest experiment this country has performed in a few years!)

Much of the nonstatistical evidence for ESP is much like my Challenger experience—anecdotal. You have a feeling about a pending situation—an accident or an illness in the family—then subsequent events validate that feeling, at least as far as *you* are concerned.

Let me give another example, far less significant and emotional than the shuttle explosion. One Saturday night several years ago, I drove a couple of friends from a faculty party in Berkeley, California, south on Highway 17; the traffic was stop-and-go, four lanes wide—after midnight! Nothing to do but inch along with the flow. Next to my pickup truck, a wild young man jockeyed a beat-up Buick for position, nearly sideswiping me as I lay on the horn. Wisely, I let the crazy driver cut in front of me and watched as he raced his eight-cylinder engine, accelerating for a few feet, then jamming on his brakes. I turned to my companions and commented, "You know, if I were that guy, I would just pull over into the divider lane and stomp it!"

Not more than ten seconds later, the driver did indeed pull into the divider and start to gun his engine; then he thought better of it and pulled back into line. I was flabbergasted! Had I somehow mentally influenced this nut to step over the line of rationality and go careening down the center of the freeway? No, I had not been able to read his mind, nor was I able to transmit my dangerous thought via ESP. What I had done was read his body language, his driving manner, and deduced what state of mind he was in and what he was likely to do. Reading other drivers' body language is one of the ways I've managed to avoid being hit while driving California's freeways all these years, a skill which I've developed and practiced. No ESP was involved.

Yet the incident, reported a bit differently, could well serve as good anecdotal evidence for precognition or ESP. Certainly, many of the anecdotal reports of ESP and precognition can be explained in much the same way: the person had some inkling that Uncle Joe was going to die, or that Cousin Billy was behaving in a way that might lead to disaster. And remember, it's only the coincidence of us thinking about such possibilities *before* the actual occurrence that makes such events significant. If I had not thought about the driver going beserk, his pulling out into the divider lane would have been of little significance to me; the fact that I thought about it beforehand as a result of observing his behavior gave the entire sequence of events a far more-than-normal significance.

Carl Jung called such significant coincidences, *synchronicities*. If people have any extrasensory perception or precognitive ability, I feel it can lie only in our ability to recognize synchronicities. No thought transference, no mysterious knowledge of the future, need be invoked as explanation— merely our own innate ability to recognize behavior patterns both consciously and subconsciously.

Entropy and ESP

If extremely weak "brain radio waves" cannot account for ESP thought transference, there is one theoretical possibility mentioned in Chapter 3: entropy, that mysterious mathematical/thermodynamic function that corresponds to the amount of order or disorder in a system. Entropy calculations are commonly used by physicists and chemists to make predictions about atomic and chemical systems (isolated groups of atoms); in fact, crystal growth rates are calculated with the aid of formulas linking energy and entropy, so science recognizes crystals as containing negative entropy (crystalline atomic structure is more "ordered" than noncrystals).

If it could be shown that the brain—being more ordered than a glob of gray mud—also has entropy associated with it, then perhaps this "brain entropy" could account for ESP in general and for crystals' enhancement of ESP in particular.

Entropy was first associated with living things by Erwin Schrodinger in his groundbreaking 1944 book, *What Is Life? The Physical Aspect of the Living Cell:* "Everything that is going on in nature means an increase of entropy and that the living being continuously increases its entropy, that is, produces positive entropy, thus approaching the state of maximum entropy, which is death. . . . The organism can remain alive only by continuously drawing negative entropy from its environment."[3]

Schrodinger called this negative life entropy *negentropy;* his theory has been alternately accepted and rejected by biologists ever since. Likewise, pure information—since it is more ordered than random gibberish—has entropy associated with it, a theory first proposed by Leo Szilard in 1929 and made a standard part of information theory by Leon Brillouin in his classic 1956 textbook, *Science and Information Theory.* A number of parapsychologists have made the theoretical leap combining life negentropy and information negentropy to come up with a theoretical model for ESP, using entropy as the transmitting force.

In the entropy model for ESP, the sender and the receiver are pictured as an isolated system: when the ESP sender thinks of a symbol to send telepathically, the brain waves become fixed on that symbol (i.e., more ordered) and thus acquire a negative entropy; the ESP receiver on the other hand generates "questing" brain-wave patterns, which are less ordered and thus have a positive entropy. Since entropy naturally flows from negative to positive, the theory goes, negative entropy then will flow from sender to receiver, carrying along the information about the symbol with it.

There is one flaw in this ESP entropy model, however; entropy levels only determine which energy or information states are possible. If several different states are all equally probable (e.g., any of five Zenner symbols), such entropy flow would not distinguish between the five possible symbols; thus the ESP entropy model leaves us right where we started: chance level of guessing the correct symbol. But if each of the symbols represents different information to the sender and thus different levels of generated negentropy, then the receiver could conceivably detect the different levels of entropy flowing from the sender, and the receiver's entropy-information levels would have to correspond to the sender's. Psychics would call this "being on the same wavelength."

Remember, all this is highly theoretical. Entropy cannot be physically seen, measured, or detected by any of our sophisticated instruments; it can only be calculated indirectly after all other parameters (energy, volume, pressure) of the system have been measured. But at least the theory gives the parapsychologists something to measure experimentally. EEG machines attached to both ESP sender and receiver can measure energy levels of their brain-wave patterns simultaneously; if the receiver's brain-wave levels go down immediately after the sender's levels go down, perhaps an entropy transfer has occurred—but the receiver still has to guess the correct symbol!

As mentioned in Chapter 3, crystals already contain negative entropy because they are highly ordered structures. For crystals to amplify ESP power, they must be capable of receiving *more* negative entropy (representing the information being transferred), then somehow retransmit an amplified amount of negentropy that still carries the original information to the receiver. This would leave the crystal in a state of decreased negative entropy and thus temporarily more disordered, which suggests another experiment for crystal workers: use X-ray diffraction methods to measure order in a crystal being used for ESP amplification. If the crystal's X-ray diffraction peaks become broadened during the experiment, then long-range order in the crystal has been affected and crystal-power advocates would have at least indirect evidence that information transfer has occurred.

As stated earlier in this chapter, I frankly doubt that ESP exists, in the physical sense of a measurable, controllable process. Under the right conditions, Jung's synchronicities might occur, which resemble ESP-like thought transfer, but I doubt that such accidentally correct guesses can be predicted, much less controlled.

In sum, ESP and other alleged parapsychological powers remain unproven and only vaguely possible theoretically. If crystal power could greatly increase ESP, that should become immediately obvious via statistical testing; otherwise such claims should be taken with a crystal of salt!

9

THE EXPERIMENTS: TESTING CRYSTAL-POWER CLAIMS

So far, we have looked at dozens of claims for crystal power and examined several theories on how crystals might conceivably cure illnesses (placebo effect), enhance ESP power (brain radio waves and entropy), and help improve psychological problems (Hawthorne effect). But the real test for any scientific theory must come via experimentation.

By their very nature, many of the claims for crystal power cannot be tested, particularly the historical claims and the spiritual claims. How can we ever test the claim that the legendary Atlanteans built the Egyptian pyramids using crystals to raise 50-ton blocks of sandstone? How can we ever test the claim that crystals can be used to communicate with disembodied spirits and "ascended masters"? What possible experiment could test the claim that "all Light, all

Life, all Intelligence is coded crystallinity . . ."?[1]

In preparing this book, my first chore was to find crystal-power claims that could be tested. Obviously, the physical claims—that crystals improve gas mileage; crystals purify water and make plants grow better—are the easiest to test, and I set about doing just that: designing experiments and purchasing supplies. The results of those physical experiments will be given shortly, along with the results of a national survey of crystal users sponsored by *Fate* magazine and *Lapidary Journal.*

But one experiment I originally wanted to run—to test my hypothesis that crystals serve as a placebo in medical claims for crystal power—proved fraught with difficulties and ethical problems. My original idea for a medical crystal power experiment was to select a group of patients with an appropriate ailment (headaches, high blood pressure, arthritis), then randomly assign these patients to two groups: (1) crystal group to be treated by crystal workers using real crystals, and (2) a placebo group to be treated by crystal workers using fake crystals made of glass to resemble the real thing. The experiment would be double-blind—that is, neither the patients nor the crystal healers would know if they were using a real crystal or not. If the real-crystal group had a significantly higher cure rate than the fake-crystal group, then we would have evidence that crystals do indeed perform better at healing than equivalent placebos, as well as evidence that crystal power does indeed exist.

Such an experiment presents many problems however:

- Medical personnel would be needed to screen potential subjects and evaluate changes in their conditions.
- The experiment would require considerable time, money, and effort.
- Creating realistic fake crystals that would fool knowledgable crystal workers is a serious obstacle because quartz can scratch glass but not vice versa, so fakes would be easy to detect.
- Ethical questions also arise: How ethical is it to treat real medical problems with not one but two suspected placebos?

Realizing such an experiment was beyond my resources and powers of deception, I decided to use a different approach and instead test my hypothesis *indirectly,* using social-science methodology; I would survey crystal workers themselves about how effective crystals are at healing. Obviously, such an approach also has limitations: crystal advocates could simply lie and claim that crystals have marvelous healing powers, or they could simply report only their successes and fail to mention failures, or they might really believe their "patients" are getting better, whereas an independent doctor might see no change; or they might simply choose patients who are likely to get better with or without treatment (like Peter Popoff ignoring the blind and the deaf).

A carefully prepared questionnaire can minimize such problems, however, by using questions that check for internal consistency and which separate respondents into "blind believers" as opposed to those who are making careful observations of their successes and failures. As we shall see shortly, I did indeed prepare such a questionnaire, which received national circulation and resulted in 190 valid responses from crystal workers and others interested in crystal power.

Before I describe the survey and my other physical experiments, however, I should set the stage by explaining how science uses experiments and surveys to test hypotheses.

Scientific Hypothesis Testing

Science is divided into two broad categories: the hard physical sciences (physics, chemistry, thermodynamics, some biology) and the so-called "soft" social sciences (sociology, psychology, psychiatry, the rest of biology). The distinction between hard and soft science boils down to *control,* and one's degree of confidence in experimental results. The physical scientist is able to control his experiments far more than a social scientist can; it is far easier to control and measure physical variables such as temperature, pressure, volume, velocity, wavelength, voltage, amperage, etc. than it is to control and measure social variables: personality, mood, hormonal changes, belief structures, job satisfaction, attitudes, reactions to drugs, susceptibility to hypnosis and placebos, and so on. The list of interesting social variables we'd like to be able to measure accurately but can't spans entire fields of study: every experiment, every paper written in these fields must deal with soft variables that can be measured only be indirectly and imperfectly.

Because hard physical variables can be accurately measured and often controlled, the physical scientist can design carefully controlled experiments that ideally limit the *uncontrolled* (dependent) variables to just one or two. In physical experiments, changes in the dependent variables are directly correlated to changes in the controlled (independent) variables. If experiments are well designed and performed, results in the hard sciences should always turn out the same from experiment to experiment, within the narrow limits of experimental error.

For instance, Freshman physics students often perform gravity experiments, say by rolling a steel ball down an incline and measuring how far the ball travels in the air before gravity brings it down to the table where carbon paper records the landing spot. If the same experiment is performed over and over, say 10 to 50 times, the carbon-paper marks will cluster symmetrically about the theoretically calculated mark, as shown in Figure 9–1. If plotted, this symmetrical error cluster will resemble what scientists call the bell curve; because of the mathematical properties of this bell curve, statisticians can tell us the likelihood or probability of any given set of experimental results. (For example, look back at Table 8–1). When results fall outside acceptable probability range (usually two standard deviations or 5% probability), results become suspect; either an unknown outside force or variable has confounded the results, or there is a mistake in measurement. For instance, if the steel ball falls consistently short of the theoretical mark, then one might suspect a magnet hidden beneath the table, or faulty measurements or procedures.

Figure 9-1: Gravity Experiment Performed by Freshman Physics Students

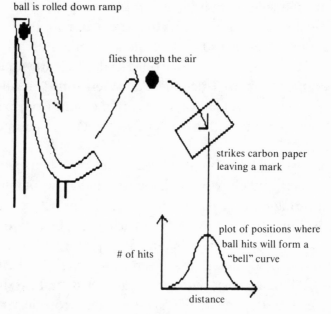

Freshman physics students often take their experiments lightly, and are famous for fudging their results so that the steel ball measurements are tightly clustered about the expected value. Physics professors have been known to flunk students whose results are too perfect, because future physicists are supposed to learn how to measure experimental error and are supposed to be ethical in their experimental measurements. Even the most carefully controlled, ideal physical experiment will contain experimental error, simply because we can't measure and control everything precisely. In the steel ball experiment, small differences in release height or the way in which the ball is released will affect how far the ball travels.

In the social sciences, this bell/error curve has become a way of life, for two reasons: (1) Social scientists must expect large errors in measuring social variables (thus, their papers are often dominated by discussions of statistics, probabilities, and validity); and (2) social scientists also use the bell curve to *infer* that their independent variables have had some effect on their dependent variables.

This latter use of the bell curve is called *hypothesis testing,* and it illustrates an essential difference between the hard and soft sciences: in the hard sciences, test variables are assumed to be directly linked—that is, a change in one variable (say, pressure or temperature) will always result in a corresponding change in the dependent variable (say, rate of chemical reaction). The independent variable is said to *cause* the dependent variable to change (the *effect*); mathematicians call this direct cause-and-effect relationship between variables a one-to-one correspondence.

Ideally, that's what all scientists are looking for in their experiments, a one-to-one correspondence between variables or a cause-and-effect relationship. The *nature* of that relationship— *how* the two variables are related—is called the *hypothesis.* The hypothesis forms the backbone of science, the starting point of the scientific method, which begins with two simple concepts: (1) *hypothesis:* a proposed cause-and-effect relationship between independent and dependent variables; and (2) *experiment:* a set of controlled procedures designed to test a hypothesis, usually by measuring independent and dependent variables.

What laymen often fail to understand about the scientific method is that the hypothesis must come first, *before* the experiments testing the hypothesis are carried out. Oddly enough, it does not matter how the scientist comes up with the hypothesis; the scientist may use logic, math, earlier observations, intuition, or even literally dream up the idea. (Many scientists have credited dreams as providing creative breakthroughs by coming up with hypotheses, most notably the case of the double-helix structure for DNA). The scientific method, then, begins with a simple two-step process: (1) proposing a hypothesis that can be tested, and (2) designing and carrying out experiments that test the hypothesis.

Once a scientist has performed his experiments and evaluated his results, he will then decide if his results support the hypothesis; otherwise, he must reject the hypothesis and accept what statisticians call the null hypothesis (that there is no cause-and-effect relationship between the variables). A good scientist, especially a good social scientist, never says that he has *proven* his hypothesis but rather that results *support* the hypothesis. Then it is up to other scientists to repeat the experiment to see if their results also support the hypothesis; this is called *replicating* the experiment. Once a hypothesis has been tested, revised, and tested again, with results consistently supporting the hypothesis, it may be raised to the status of a *theory* (e.g., the theory of evolution), and if a theory is found to be universally applicable, it may be declared a scientific *law* (e.g., the law of gravity).

Crystal-Power Hypotheses

A key fact to remember about hypotheses is that they must be *testable,* which means that variables can be measured and experiments designed. That a hypothesis must be testable may seem self-evident, but many would-be scientists forget that basic fact and come up with hypotheses which cannot be tested, as in the case of a Russian professor, Tchijewsky, who tried to prove that all history, all historical events—epidemics, wars, social revolutions—can be linked to sunspot activity.[2]

At first, Professor Tchijewsky's hypothesis seems testable enough since all that is required is to match historical dates (dependent variable) with sunspot activity on those dates (independent variable), but upon closer examination the hypothesis is riddled with flaws:

- Prior to 1860, astronomers lacked the equipment to observe and count sunspots; no data exists before 1860.
- Lacking data, Tchijewsky used the average 11–year sunspot cycle to correlate with events; actual sunspot activity does not follow a precise 11–year cycle but may vary from 7 to 14 years.
- It is a rare year that doesn't see some historical upheaval somewhere on the planet; the researcher only has to choose which events to include in his study.

Tchijewsky's sunspot hypothesis suffers from two other major flaws, which it shares with many of the claims for crystal power:

- Such claims are too broad, too sweeping in their generalizations; Tchijewsky's hypothesis tries to explain all of man's major ills with one simple theory using one simple independent variable (number of sunspots).
- Such claims hypothesize cause-and-effect relationships where none are known to exist; scientists have found no mechanism whereby sunspots could cause an outbreak of smallpox or start a revolution; likewise, scientists see no way crystals can amplify thoughts, improve gas mileage, or help plants grow faster and stronger.

Hypotheses, however, do not necessarily need to make sense to be testable. When Galileo proposed in 1604 that that the speed at which a falling object strikes the earth depends only on its height at the beginning of its fall—and not on the weight of the object as was commonly thought—his hypothesis did not conform to contemporary thought, but simple experiments easily bore him out. When Einstein proposed in 1916 that matter and energy are functionally equivalent via the formula, $E = mc^2$, the hypothesis did not make much sense at the time, but later the atomic bomb dramatically supported his hypothesis.

Many of the claims for crystal power do not make sense to scientists, but at least some of them can be tested. Looking back at the dozens of claims for crystal power listed in Chapter 2, we can construct a corresponding list of testable crystal-power hypotheses:

Physical Crystal-Power Hypotheses

1. Crystals possess an energy field with a one-foot radius.
2. Quartz crystal attached to the outside of a fuel line will improve a vehicle's gas mileage.
3. Quartz crystal placed in tap water will purify the water.
4. Such crystal-purified water will increase plant growth.
5. Quartz crystals placed near plants will increase growth.

Medical Crystal-Power Hypotheses

6. Crystals heal specific parts of the body when worn next to them.
7. Different colored crystals can heal different parts of the body.
8. Crystals amplify healing thoughts, which can cure patients.

Parapsychological Crystal-Power Hypotheses

9. Crystals increase parapsychological powers (ESP, clairvoyance, and precognition).

These nine hypotheses for crystal power are reasonably

testable using the scientific method. The independent variable is merely the presence or absense of crystals and remains the same for all nine hypotheses. In each case, the dependent variable can be measured (e.g., energy, gas mileage, impurities in water, plant growth, cure rate, success with Zener cards, etc.).

I would add one further hypothesis to the list of medical hypotheses:

Placebo Hypothesis for Medical Crystal-Power

10. Medical treatments using crystals will have a success rate equal to an equivalent placebo treatment (approximately a 35% success rate).

Of these ten hypotheses, I have personally run experiments to test the physical hypotheses 2, 3, and 4 (gas mileage, water purity, and plant growth). The placebo hypothesis, number 10, I have tested indirectly by formulating a corollary hypothesis, which could be tested by surveying crystal workers who claimed varying degrees of success using crystals to heal themselves and others. Results were not always what I expected (particularly in the survey of crystal users), but the experiments illustrate some of the problems that can arise and that may have led less careful experimenters awry.

The Experiments

Gas-Mileage Experiment

Since it seemed the most straightforward and easiest experiment to perform, I decided first to test physical hypothesis 2, proposed by Dael Walker, director of the Crystal Awareness Institute of Pacheco, California. I telephoned Mr. Walker, who suggested details of the experiment, "Use a cheap, natural quartz crystal, about 2½ inches long, about as big around as your finger. Attach the crystal to the fuel line near the carburetor with a hose clamp or electrician's tape. Make sure the point of the crystal points toward the carburetor. You don't have to 'clear' or energize the crystal, although I have since done that with some small gains in mileage. Maximum gain in gas mileage I've seen is 35%; minimum gain is 10%; average gain in gas mileage runs 15% to 20%. An elderly couple in Costa Mesa claims 50% improvement."[3]

Dael Walker tested gas mileage on fairly short drives (e.g., from Pacheco to Sacramento, less than 100 miles), driving one direction without the crystal, then retracing his drive with the crystal attached to the fuel line, maintaining the same approximate speed and style of driving in both directions. This method appears subject to error: How could you be sure that speed and driving style were constant? What if you got stuck in a traffic jam? What about headwinds and tailwinds? What if one direction is uphill and the other downhill?

I decided that a more accurate test—and the only one that counts to motorists—would be to average gas mileage over long periods of day-to-day driving. I decided I would run the test by tankfuls, alternately attaching and removing the crystal after each fill-up. My gas mileage experiment spanned more than a month, with five separate fill-ups and measurement of gas mileage. (See Appendix A for the complete written report of the experiment as it took place.) Table 9-1 summarizes the results; Figure 9-2 is a photo of the crystal attached to the carburetor fuel line.

TABLE 9-1
Gas-Mileage Experiment Results

Normal Mileage Runs			Crystal Mileage Runs		
miles	gals	mpg	miles	gals	mpg
242.0	10.8	22.41	240.8	10.01	24.06
293.1	10.1	29.02	164.4	7.56	21.75
535.1	20.9	25.60	405.2	17.57	23.06

Table 9-1 shows that my 1984 Mazda truck obtained higher mileage *without* the crystal attached (25.6 mpg compared to 23.06 mpg), mainly due to the high mileage (29.02 mpg compared to EPA estimate mileage of 26 mpg) obtained

Figure 9-2: Crystal Gas Mileage Experiment
photo by Michael Gelic

mostly during a long freeway drive up and back to my sailboat (San Jose to Richmond). Lowest mileage was obtained with crystal attached (21.75 mpg), mainly due to being stuck in rush-hour traffic one afternoon. Overall average mileage (with and without crystal) was 24.44 mpg, compared to EPA estimated mileage of 26 mpg—not bad for a four-year-old truck with over 50,000 miles!

But, unfortunately, the crystal didn't help; in fact, my best mileage (without crystal) was 33% better than my worst mileage (with crystal). Had those been my only two runs, I might have concluded that crystals actually *decrease* mileage! In fact, average mileage was 24.44 +/- 3.29 mpg; that is, actual mileage varied 13% above or below the average value—very close to Walker's claimed average gain of 15%.

In short, small differences in driving conditions can easily result in 30% gains between one mileage measurement and another. It would be easy for crystal-power advocates anxious to prove that crystal power increases gas mileage subconsciously to drive more cautiously and obtain 10%, 15%, or even 30% better mileage.

Certainly, my own gas-mileage experiment does not support the hypothesis that a crystal attached to the fuel line improves mileage.

Water-Purity Experiment

Several crystal-power authors claim that crystals purify water and/or enhance plant growth. One such is Dael Walker, who claimed in a telephone conversation that he had performed such experiments, even to submitting water samples to laboratories for testing. I decided to use Walker's methodology for both the water-purity and plant-growth experiments. Walker claimed that placing a large quartz crystal in a jug of water will purify it, removing impurities and softening the water so it would taste "flat."[4]

The major source of hardness in tap water is carbonates (CO_3), combined with calcium and magnesium ions (called "temporary hardness").[5] I checked with a local water-testing laboratory, and they agreed that hardness would be the primary test for water purity and, since just a few laboratory tests would run into hundreds of dollars, I purchased a Hach Hardness Test Kit and ran more than a dozen water hardness tests of a variety of water samples; the results are shown in Table 9–2.

TABLE 9–2
Water-Hardness Tests
(in grains of CaCO₃ per gal.)

	Ionized Water	½ Tap/Ion. Water	Crystal Water	Tap Water	Aquarium Water
	0	4	—	8	22
			8	7	
			8	8	
			6½	6½	
			6½	7	
av:	0	4	7.25	7.30	22

Table 9–2 shows that the Hardness Test Kit proved fairly accurate: purified water (common steam-iron ionized bottled water) tested zero, while a half-and-half mixture of tap water and purified water tested at 4 gpg and a sample of tap water tested at 8 gpg. No matter how long the quartz crystal was left to try and purify the jug of tap water, crystal water always tested the same as tap water, within experimental error.

My experiment did not support the hypothesis that crystals can purify water, but perhaps the crystal water would still help plants grow better. I proceeded with the next experiment.

Crystal/Marigold Experiment

Biological experiments can always prove tricky, and this one proved no exception. The nature of the experiment imposed some restrictions: the plants could receive no rain water, so the plants would have to be kept inside as long as there was a threat of rain. I would have to keep the plants carefully separated so that the crystal-treated plants received only crystal-purified water and the control plants only tap water.

I decided to use that old biology lab standby, the marigold, and purchased a package of dwarf-marigold seeds, plus two dozen sprouting pots (in 2 separate 12-packs) and a bag of sterilized soil. Normally I use natural compost to grow plants, but for the experiment I wanted to eliminate weed seeds, so I purchased a standard budget brand of "soil," which proved to be large organic chips.

I took photographs of the starting equipment (see Figure 9–3), then started the marigold seeds, one per sprouting cup, being careful that the control batch only got tap water and the test batch was watered with only "crystal-purified" water. The complete write-up of the experiment appears in Appen-

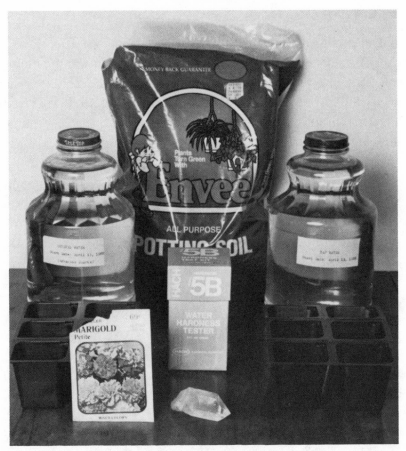

Figure 9-3: Crystal Marigold Experimental Setup
photo by Michael Gelic

dix B. Note that, at first, the "crystal-water" seedlings showed a slight edge over the controls (one more sprouted than the tap-water batch), then the tap-water control plants gained an edge; at the end of the experiment four months later, both batches of plants had bloomed and showed remarkably equal growth.

In fact, the biology of the experiment and the problems encountered proved more interesting than the results. The seeds all sprouted well, but only 15 of the 24 seeds survived the first month. I began to suspect that the sterile organic soil lacked nutrients and transplanted 12 of the healthiest into slightly larger styrofoam cups with natural compost. At the time of transplant, the seedlings' roots were long and stringy, as if they were searching for some decent soil. Soon after transplanting, all plants perked up and grew fairly well until blooming. As shown in Figure 9–4, the "crystal marigolds" grew no better than the "tap-water marigolds."

Figure 9-4: Results of Crystal Marigold Experiment
photo by Lawrence Jerome

Besides not supporting the hypothesis that "crystal-purified" water helps plants grow better, the experiment also demonstrates how slight changes in local environment (or perhaps just the luck of genetics) can favor one plant over another—perhaps one receives better light, a little more moisture, or more nutrients. However, with a large enough sample, such differences will average out, and "crystal-powered" plants will be seen to grow no better than plants getting normal care.

Crystal Power Survey

Lacking the medical resources and ethical justification for directly testing the placebo hypothesis, number 10, I decided to try an indirect test of the hypothesis, using social-science survey methodology, the same methodology I teach in a Research and Statistics course for the University of San Francisco's College of Professional Studies.

First, I needed to revise my hypothesis to make it suitable for testing via questions on a survey questionnaire. (Statisticians call this *operationalizing variables*). I reasoned that, if crystals are acting as placebos in crystal power medical treatments, then the patient must know about the crystal being used in an attempt to cure him or her (just as voodoo victims must be aware that black magic is being performed against them). Furthermore, I reasoned, the placebo should be more effective if the patient participates in the "crystal-healing" ritual or ceremony. (See Appendix C for a complete account of the statistical reasoning and planning that went into this experiment.)

Thus, the placebo hypothesis can be stated as a corollary hypothesis: H(A2): Those who note that crystals work best while the recipient is present are really noticing the placebo effect, and thus will find that crystal "energies" do not work well at a distance, while those who believe they can affect recipients not present will also believe the crystal "energies" can extend almost any distance.

I sent copies of my questionnaire to *Fate* magazine and *Lapidary Journal,* asking their assistance with the survey in return for an article giving the results. *Fate*'s managing editor, Jerome Clark, kindly accepted my offer and ran "The *Fate* Crystal Survey" in the August 1988 issue.[6] The *Fate* questionnaire is shown in Figure 9–5.

Lapidary Journal did not run the actual questionnaire, but carried a notice concerning the survey at the end of an article on crystal power; interested readers could send for the questionnaire, but only a dozen did so.[7]

As the filled-in questionnaires arrived, the raw data was input into an XT–compatible computer using the statistical software package, Statpac Gold, which was then used to perform the statistical analyses given in Appendix D.

Between *Fate* and *Lapidary Journal,* I received a total of 190 responses to my questionniare: 178 (93.7%) came from *Fate* readers and 12 (6.3%) from *Lapidary Journal* readers. Nearly half of the respondents (47.1%) said they had been interested in crystals more than five years, while only 11.1%

Figure 9-5: *Fate* Crystal Survey Questionnaire

THE **FATE** CRYSTAL SURVEY

I N ASSOCIATION with Prof. Lawrence Jerome of the University of San Francisco, FATE is conducting a survey of our readers' use of crystals and crystal power. The results of this survey will appear in an article in a future issue.

Your answers will be kept strictly confidential. The completed questionnaire should be sent to Lawrence Jerome, 10301 Serrano Ct., San Jose, Calif. 95127.

1. How did you become interested in crystals and crystal power?
   ___ through friends ___ reading articles ___ Shirley MacLaine TV show
   ___ psychic fair ___ other: _____

2. How long have you been interested in crystals?
   ___ less than 1 year ___ 1 to 2 years ___ 2 to 5 years ___ more than 5 years

3. Sex: ___ M ___ F

4. Age: ___ under 18 ___ 18-25 ___ 26-40 ___ 40-60 ___ over 60

5. Do you own any crystals? ___ yes ___ no
   If yes, what is the value of your crystals?
   ___ $0-$50 ___ $50-$100 ___ $100-$200 ___ $200-$500 ___ over $500

6. Do you wear crystals? ___ yes ___ no
   If yes, how often?
   ___ once a month or less ___ once a week ___ daily ___ always

7. Would you describe yourself as a "crystal worker"? ___ yes ___ no
   If yes, choose the categories that best describe your work:
   ___ self healing ___ healing others ___ healing at a distance
   ___ meditation and/or self improvement ___ astral projection/travel
   ___ ESP (telepathy, clairvoyance) ___ channeling
   ___ influencing people and events ___ other: _____

8. In your experience, do crystals work best when the recipient of its energies (healings, ESP, etc.) participate in the energizing? ___ yes ___ no
   How successful have you been when recipients do *not* take part in the energizing?
   ___ not at all ___ somewhat successful ___ very successful

9. When you are trying to influence others (ESP, projections, healings) what is the maximum effective distance between you and your subject?
   ___ subject must be in same room ___ 100 feet ___ 1 mile
   ___ 100 miles ___ no limit. Other: _____

10. Do you tell recipients you are directing crystal energies toward them?
    ___ yes ___ no ___ sometimes

11. Would you be willing to participate in scientific tests of crystal power?
    ___ yes ___ no
    If yes, include pertinent information:

    Name _____

    Address _____

    City _____ State/Zip _____

    Phone _____

had been interested for less than one year. Thus, the survey sample reached its intended population: crystal workers most interested and knowledgeable about the subject. In fact, two-thirds of the respondents (68.4%) described themselves as "crystal workers," and nearly three-fourths (73%) regularly wear crystals—40.9% always wear a crystal.

Appendix D gives the complete results of the Crystal-Power Survey. What interests us most here is the results of the hypothesis testing: Did those crystal workers who felt crystals work best when recipients participate in the procedure also find distance a critical factor? In testing this hypothesis, Questions 8 and 10, shown in Figure 9–5, serve as the independent variables, while Question 9 is the dependent variable.

Almost two-thirds of the surveyed crystal workers (64.5%) reported "Yes," their recipients of crystal energies participated in the crystal "energizing," while 40% said, "No," they don't tell recipients they are directing crystal energies toward them. Of the 113 respondents who answered the second part of Question 8 ("How successful have you been when recipients *do not* take part in the energizing?"), 15.9% reported no success, half (50.4%) reported some success, and one-third (33.6%) claimed to be very successful.

A total of 138 respondents answered Question 9 (the dependent variable): 18.8% reported that crystals work best when the recipient of crystal "energies" is in the same room, while a surprising 58% felt that crystal "energies" have "no limit" to the distance at which they will work.

"No limit" to the distance! Indeed, several respondents

wrote additional comments backing up their distance claims:

- "Have worked 1,000 miles."
- "I have communicated between linked spheres across the United States—specifically, from Alexandria, Va. to Los Angeles, Calif."
- "There is no limit in the distance."
- "I actively do healings every day on my customers and so far have done six long distance healings with complete success."
- "I prefer to do healing at a distance, and not always with the other person aware of what is happening."
- "20 miles."
- "Never tried over 10 miles."
- "I have detected storms at least 300 miles from here . . . this also holds very true when UFOs are in the area . . . I am 285 miles from Shirley MacLain's (sic) new Metaphysical area; I can well detect it by rotating the generator until it starts to glow."
- "I do not believe distance to be a factor. A thousand miles or one mile; if it is going to work, it will work."
- "Have only worked within established geographical bounds of lower 48 states."
- "Dallas to California."
- "Distance no factor."

Distance is no factor? To a scientist, this is a logical impossibility: every force and energy known to man diminishes with distance, in general obeying what's known as the inverse-square law. For instance, the force of gravity varies as the square of the distance between the two bodies, and the intensity of light from a point source will be one-fourth as strong at twice the distance; even laser beams spread out and diminish in power at long distances.

To the scientist, then, the claim that crystal power has no limit on distance can mean only one of two things: (1) Crystal power and crystal energies do not exist physically but result from psychological influences between crystal worker and subject, or (2) crystal power and crystal energies must work like a laser, concentrated into a narrow, parallel beam aimed directly between the crystal and its intended recipient.

Conclusion (1) obviously supports my hypothesis that crystals act as placebos. Conclusion (2) presents another logical difficulty: How can a quartz crystal "know" exactly where an intended recipient is located in order to direct a narrow beam of crystal energy straight to the intended target thousands of miles away? Although crystals can and do serve as lasers as explained in Chapter 5, the resulting laser light-beam is well understood by scientists; the source of the laser's energy must be pumped into the crystal at considerable expense and effort, and at considerable loss of efficiency. Crystal workers are claiming to be able to do much the same—for free!

My crystal-survey questionnaire, then, was successful in separating those who claim crystal power has no distance limit, from those who find crystals only work when the recipient is in the same room. To test my corollary hypothesis, then, I used the standard chi-square test (which measures if the observed distribution differs significantly from the expected normal distribution) between Questions 8 and 9, and between Questions 10 and 9. The results were mixed (computer chi-square results are included in Appendix D):

- Question 8 (recipients participate) by Question 9 (maximum distance): chi-square = 4.34, with a probability of chance = .502; does not support the hypothesis.
- Question 10 (tell recipient) by Question 9 (maximum distance): chi-square = 35.416, with a probability of chance = .000; strongly supports the hypothesis.

In short, those crystal workers who separate clients by whether or not they participate in the energizing *do not* see distance as a limiting factor, while those who tell their clients they will be directing crystal energies toward them *do* see distance as a limiting factor. One chi-square test strongly supports my corollary-placebo hypothesis, while the other chi-square test does not.

One further statistical test, Spearman's Rank Order Correlation Coefficient, tells us how strongly Questions 10 and 9 are correlated; the final results in Appendix D show a value of rs = 0.3753 with a probability of .000—not a strong correlation but a significant one. (A Spearman's r of 0.3753 corresponds to a 14% "strength of correlation," which means that 14% of the cases are accounted for by the correlation.)

Finally, as already pointed out in Chapter 6, the Crystal-Power Survey provides some interesting statistics about the uses to which crystal workers put their crystals (Question 7 on the questionnaire), as shown in the multiresponse analysis given in Table 9-3.

TABLE 9-3
Multiresponse Analysis: Uses of Crystals

Number of cases: 190	No.	Per cent
Q7b: Self-healing	106	55.8
Q7c: Healing others	73	38.4
Q7d: Healing at distance	54	28.4
Q7e: Meditation/self-improvement	110	57.9
Q7f: Astral projection	36	18.9
Q7g: ESP	65	34.2
Q7h: Channeling	37	19.5
Q7i: Influencing	41	21.6
Q7j: Other	47	24.7

Note: Percentages add up to more than 100% because of multiple responses.

Chapter 6 noted how the percentage of those who use crystal power for healing others (38.4%) closely matches the average placebo effect response rate (35%) and that the percentages for self-healing (55.8%) and meditation/self-improvement (57.9%) are within the observed ranges for the psychological Hawthorne effect (50%–80%).

Results of the Crystal-Power Survey, then, support in several different ways the hypothesis that the placebo effect (along with the Hawthorne effect) accounts for any claimed successes for crystal power. The so-called power of crystals would seem to exist only in the minds (or subconscious) of those who believe.

10

THE ULTIMATE
PLACEBO EFFECT

Our search for crystal power has led us into many fascinating fields: prehistoric shamanism, Middle-Ages crystal gazing, parapsychology, modern medicine, and scientific hypothesis testing. Along the way, we have learned that a controversy is brewing among doctors about the placebo effect and what it means. We've learned about the Hawthorne effect and how people's natural urge to please can affect their performance and psychological state of mind. We've looked at ancient superstitions and modern legends, talked about yoga, acupuncture, and faith-healing, and discussed theories about how the mind operates. At the same time, we've looked at what crystals really are, how they are formed, and how modern science uses crystals in today's high-tech gadgetry. I've performed experiments, surveyed crystal workers, and interviewed experts and amateurs.

Along the way, I have collected considerable evidence that crystal power and crystal energies do not exist physically but rather are manifestations of the placebo effect (for medical claims) and/or the Hawthorne effect (for psychological claims). When crystal workers use crystals as part of a medical therapy, they automatically invoke the placebo effect, which will produce a 35% success rate for a wide variety of illnesses—just as doctors have done throughout the ages using as placebos bread and sugar pills. When crystal workers use crystals as part of a program of psychological improvement, they automatically invoke not only the placebo effect but also the Hawthorne effect, which can yield a rate of improvement of from 50% to 80%.

Small wonder that crystal workers become convinced that their crystals actually possess power and energy. Such successes might turn the head of even the most hardened skeptic—if he or she were unaware of scientific testing methods, controlled experimentation, and the placebo effect. Likewise, for those unfamiliar with relaxation methods, yoga, and biofeedback, the use of crystals for self-improvement, visualization techniques, and right-brain intuitive thinking might border on the magical. And for those who already believe that ESP and other parapsychological powers exist, the boost that visualization and increased alpha brain-wave patterns give to picturing symbols and thoughts might well convince them that crystals can amplify such powers.

Today's New Age practitioners may not have discovered crystal power but rather have rediscovered one of man's oldest secrets: the power of the placebo.

As we saw in Chapter 2, however, the claims for crystal

power extend far beyond what might conceivably be explained by the simple placebo effect—or even the placebo effect plus the Hawthorne effect. When crystal workers believe they can talk to God and spiritual masters inside their crystals, such notions move into the realm of religion. When crystal workers believe they can influence events and obtain wealth and possessions by ritualistically asking their "crystal spirit guide" over and over to grant their wishes, crystals have become sacred objects and the rituals have become prayers. And when crystal workers focus on their crystals to produce visions and relaxation, the crystals act as *mandalas,* geometric patterns used by Eastern mystics as a focus for meditation and prayer.

This latter religious use of crystals suggests that yet a third effect be added to the two we've already discussed: the so-called totem effect. All religions have totems of some sort or other—huge carvings, candles, paintings, sacred books, altars, crosses, engraved plates, and ancient walls. These serve as a focal point for worship and prayerful thoughts. Religious totems help the faithful focus their thoughts, their visions, their hopes; in a psychological sense, religious totems help induce the proper state of mind for absorbing religious teachings and achieving what experts call the "religious experience." Any object then, which enhances religious thinking and experience may be said to produce the totem effect.

Crystals—because they are beautiful and shaped in regular patterns—may be regarded as mysterious objects and used to invoke the totem effect. At least one New Age author acknowledges: "Although many people have taken to wearing crystals on certain parts of their bodies and meditating with specific colors for desired ends, the most that can be claimed for such uses is that they function as totems—that is, the personal belief in their effectiveness may empower an individual to achieve certain results either in life or in the spiritual growth process."[1]

While I would consider this definition of crystals as totems too broad ("to achieve certain results in life" corresponds to the placebo or Hawthorne effect), the idea that crystals can function as "totems . . . in the spiritual growth process" closely matches my own definition.

Our search for crystal power has come almost full circle. When I first began research for this book, I had only a vague idea why I considered crystal power as an ultimate placebo effect. I had only a vague concept that placebos were related to the Hawthorne effect and had no inkling that the Hawthorne effect had been extended to psychiatric treatments. What I now call the totem effect I originally thought of as a "mandala effect." With research comes knowledge and with writing comes understanding. I learned a great deal in putting this book together, and I hope you, the reader, have too. In many respects, my original thesis that crystal power acts as a sort of ultimate placebo effect has turned out to be more accurate than I could have hoped. When I look back at my original proposal, I'm amazed at how closely the finished product follows that proposal.

In short, I'm surprised that the original concept hung together so well, especially after my research discovered so much controversy brewing over the placebo effect. I was surprised to find that the placebo effect accounts for an average 35% cure rate for many illnesses. (I had expected something more like a 15% cure rate.) Also, I was surprised to find other writers associating the placebo and Hawthorne effects, especially in the psychiatric realm. I haven't tried to present all the modern medical theories regarding placebos (mainly because they're couched in incomprehensible jargon), but they number in the dozens.

Some doctors have tried to subdivide the placebo response into physiological reactions (much as I tried to do with the Hawthorne effect in Chapter 6), while others suggest that the placebo effect is a mere statistical aberration (statistical regression: the tendency for extreme cases to return to the norm); and of course there is also that old medical standby, spontaneous remission, often mentioned in association with the placebo effect.

Psychologists, on the other hand, couch their theories about the placebo effect in totally different terms, talking about "transitional states," attitudes, and authority figures.

I don't know if all these theories and classification schemes help us understand the placebo effect and its counterparts, but the evidence seems clear that the placebo effect *does* exist and has a real effect on people's health and psychological state of mind. So far, what the precise mind/body mechanism is that translates a belief and faith in a placebo into physical cures remains a mystery. Much more research and experimentation is required to untangle the web linking thought and emotional state to the biochemistry of the body, which ultimately produces the physical cure.

Since crystal power exhibits all three effects (placebo, Hawthorne, and totem), it functions as an ultimate placebo effect. In other words, different patients may respond differently to the same crystal-power treatment: one may respond as if the crystal were a standard placebo sugar pill, while another patient may respond to the spiritual (totemic) aspect of crystal power, and yet a third patient may respond by wanting to please the crystal worker (Hawthorne effect).

Perhaps that is why prehistoric shamans, witch doctors, and medicine men were successful for thousands of years: they used treatments that combined all three effects; in short, they had discovered—whether consciously or not—the ultimate placebo effect long before the New Age and modern crystal power. The task for modern science, medicine, and psychology is to learn the precise mechanisms and how we can put this ultimate placebo effect to good practical use, whether through biofeedback techniques, relaxation and visualization techniques, or by developing a whole new approach to controlling the mind/body interface that affects our health and well-being.

I'm not suggesting that our modern, drug-oriented medicine should be abandoned—far from it. The reason we have drugs is because they *are* more effective than placebos, but what about cases and diseases which do not respond to drugs? Shouldn't we try to fill in those gaps, perhaps add a bit of preventive medicine, by understanding and using placebos, totems, and the Hawthorne effect? Crystal power, at least for most of us who remain skeptical, is obviously not the answer, but it may help point the way toward the ultimate placebo effect.

APPENDIX A

Gas-Mileage Experiment

D**ate:** 4/18/88. Started the Crystal Gas Mileage Experiment on Saturday. First I gave the truck a needed oil and oil filter change, then removed the air cleaner so I could see where the fuel line to the carburetor is. There are two fuel lines, running side by side, so I took the large Arkansas crystal and placed it in the middle of the 2 lines; took photographs; then taped the crystal in place with electrician's tape; took more photographs; filled up the tank; reset the trip mileage to zero.

Plan: Instead of running short, set courses up and back as Walker did (which is subject to many possible errors), I plan to drive normally to get average gas mileage under normal conditions. While this is also subject to errors, the errors will tend to cancel out statistically; average long-term mileage tends to be remarkably constant. After a couple of hundred miles, I'll remove the crystal and refill the tank to get mileage without the crystal.

Update: 4/26/88. After driving a week and a half with the crystal attached, I refilled the tank today.

Crystal Power Mileage: 240.8 miles @ 10.01 gals = 24.06 mpg

EPA Estimated MPG: 26 mpg. Not bad for a 4-year old truck with nearly 50,000 miles on it: still getting 93% of EPA estimated mileage! Removed crystal and ready for mileage test without crystal power.

Update: 5/7/88. After driving a week and a half without the crystal attached I refilled the tank.

Normal Mileage: 242.0 miles @ 10.8 gals = 22.41 mpg

% Difference: 7%, *Crystal mileage* over *normal mileage.*

Note: Had to fill up at a different gas station, which may help account for difference; also, I was caught in stop-and-go traffic on 101 for 30 minutes coming home Thursday, which can significantly lower gas mileage. Now, I'll reattach the crystal, and repeat the experiment.

Update: 5/20/88.

Crystal Mileage: 164.4 miles @ 7.56 gals = 21.75 mpg

% Difference: -3%, *Crystal mileage* under *normal mileage.*

Note: Truck was in shop last week to have transmission overhauled, which obviously didn't affect mileage since, if anything, should have improved it. Filled up at usual Rotten Robbie station, same pump as first time. Driving was standard: several trips to Cupertino, considerable local milage, very little stop and go. Tomorrow's trip to the boat in Richmond should give good freeway mileage.

Update: 5/27/88.

Normal Mileage: 293.1 miles @ 10.1 gals = 29.02 mpg.

Note: As I predicted, the long freeway trip up to the boat (plus 2 trips to Santa Clara and 2 trips to Cupertino) netted much better mileage, in fact, 12% better than the EPA estimated 26 mpg.

APPENDIX B

Crystal Water/Plant Experiment

D**ate:** 4/13/88. Started the Crystal Water Testing and Plant-Growing Experiment suggested by Dael Walker.

Steps:
1. Washed and dried 2 identical 2-quart apple-juice bottles; labeled one "crystal water" and the other "tap water."
2. Rinsed the large Arkansas quartz crystal in running cold and hot tap water to wash off any sediment and dirt, not to "clear" the crystal, and then dried it.
3. Took photographs of empty bottles along with crystal (roll 13, shots 1-4).
4. Carefully placed crystal in bottle labeled "crystal water," then filled both bottles with sink tap water (after first running water for several minutes to be sure we were getting fresh water); capped both bottles.
5. Took photographs of filled bottles (1 with crystal inside); since I used a clean knife to position crystal for photographic purposes, I also stirred the empty bottle with the same knife several times, so both bottles got the same treatment with the exception of the crystal.

161

6. Carefully placed both bottles well out of direct sun in the garage.

Observations: 4/14/88, 16 hours after start. Bottle with crystal contains more bubbles (some on crystal, but most on bottle sides) than bottle without crystal.

Planned Steps:
1. Arrange for laboratory testing of the water next week.
2. Purchase 2 identical plant-starter containers with 10 to 12 individual pots; purchase sterile potting soil and package of marigold seeds (traditional experimental plants; individual seeds are easy to separate).
3. Plant one Marigold seed per individual pot; water 1 container with "crystal water," the other with "tap water" from the two bottles above. Dael said give the crystal 2 days to a week; I should start the plants about Monday.

Experimental Goals: According to Dael Walker, the "crystal water" should taste sweeter, better, and should test purer (less hard, less impurities) than the "tap water." Plants started and grown with "crystal water" should grow faster and better than plants grown with "tap water." With this experimental setup, I'll be able to tell if there's any difference in the number of plants sprouting, and of those sprouting, which grow better.

Update on Testing: Since having two water samples tested by a lab was going to cost hundreds of dollars, I bought a Hach Water Hardness Test Kit and general-purpose pH test papers at the Science

Shop (total cost: $19.15). So far I have tested three base samples:

1. Aquarium water: 22 grains per gallon.
2. Tap water (fresh from tap): 8 grains per gallon.
3. Purified water (de-ionized Lady Lee brand): 0 grains per gallon (turned blue without adding any tritant reagant).

So, certainly, the Hardness Test Kit gives results that are in the right ballpark! I may be able to check with San Jose Water Company to see what hardness value they generally find.

4. As a test of the kit's accuracy, I mixed a half-half vial of tap water and purified water and sure enough: 4 grains per gallon!

So the kit measures hardness very accurately. Since Walker claims the crystal purifies water, removing impurities, and makes it taste flat, hardness should be the best test. (Mr. MacIntosh of MacIntosh Labs agreed.)

Update: 4/15/88.

Experiment: Purchased the supplies for this experiment as described above, except that the pots are plastic, not peat, a bit larger than the ones I had seen before but was unable to buy. Soil is Envee and seeds Petite Mixed Colors Marigolds. Took photographs before and after planting, one seed per pot. Presoaked soil in pots before covering and planting.

1. 2½ cups of water each set of pots: 20 ounces, 4/15/88
2. Pots placed together on office window sill until threat of rain passes
3. Tested water hardness of both bottles, 4/15/88:
   - Tap water: 7 gpg

- Crystal water: 8 gpg
4. pH tests:
  - Tap water: 6
  - Crystal water: 6
  - Aquarium water: 5

Update: 4/21/88. Marigold experiment has been going very well; whenever the sun has been out, I've carried the two plant containers out and placed them on the umbrella table to get full morning sun (seed packet recommends at least a half day of sun). Whenever there's been a threat of rain, I've brought the containers inside to my office window sill, where they still get a fair amount of afternoon sun.

Results to Date: On 4/21/88, the first marigold seedling was up— in the crystal-water container! At noon, I watered both containers, each with ½ cup of corresponding water from tap-water and crystal-water jugs. After watering (which settled down some of the dry loose soil on top), several more marigold seedlings became apparent:

Sprouting Results: 4/21/88, 4:30 pm:
- Crystal-water container: 3½ marigolds (½ indicates bent stem appearing)
- Tap-water container: 2½ marigolds

Update: 4/26/88. Watered the marigolds again yesterday, same 1/2 cup of appropriate water per container.

Sprouting Results: 4/26/88, 8:30 am:
- Crystal-water container: 7 marigolds
- Tap-water container: 6 marigolds

Water-Hardness Test:
- Crystal water: 8 gpg
- Tap water: 8 gpg

Update: 5/2/88. Watered 4/30/88: 1 cup each container. Watered 5/2/88: 1 cup each container.

Sprouting Results: 5/2/88, 3:45 pm:
- Crystal-water container: 7 marigolds
- Tap-water container: 7½ marigolds

Note: Sun has been out much stronger last few days; containers require much more water. In terms of growth, crystal-water marigolds look slightly ahead of tap-water marigolds, with larger primary leaves; still too soon to measure height.

Update: 5/7/88. Watered ½ cup each container.

Sprouting Results: 5/7/88, 11:00 am:
- Crystal-water container: 7 marigolds, growing strongly
- Tap-water container: 6 marigolds, growing strongly + 2 struggling seedlings

Note: Past week has been cloudy and overcast, with periodic sprinkles; had to keep plants on office window sill; only the half of containers closest to window were dry and needed water.

Update: 5/10/88. Setback: This morning, one of the tap-water plants was drooping and near death, perhaps from lack of water, perhaps damaged when I closed the drapes last night, though I can't see any damage with the magnifying glass. So I gave both containers a thorough watering of 1½ cups, then placed the plants out in the morning sun on the patio where I think I'll leave them now that all threat of rain is over for now. Then I refilled both jugs with cold tap water. The two struggling seedlings in the tap-water container have both died.

Growth Results: 5/10/88, 11:00 am: The two tallest, strongest plants are in the tap-water container.

For the Initial-Hardness Test, I refilled both jugs; each tested 6½ gpg.

Update: 5/19/88. The patio turned out to be too severe an environment, with too much hot sun all day long, so I've moved both containers into the greenhouse, where they get filtered sun or shade all day long. All of which points out that *local environment* is far more important to plants than the quality of the water they receive. Watered today, 1 full cup each container. One of the crystal-water marigolds died, cause unknown. All others seem to be doing well.

Growth Results: 5/19/88, 4:00 pm:
- Tap-water marigolds: 5 plants; 2 = 1″ tall, 3 = ½″.
- Crystal-water marigolds: 6 plants; 3 = ¾″; 3 = ½″

Update: 7/11/88. Transplanted the 3 strongest marigolds from each of the 2 groups (total of 6 plants) into styrofoam cups using compost to fill. As I suspected, all plants had long roots extending into bottom of planter—but no solid root ball—as if the roots were searching for some needed nutrient not provided by that sterile, all-organic potting soil. Left 2 plants from each group (4 total) in original plastic planters.

Took photographs before and after transplant; tap water plants measurably doing about 20% better.

Update: 7/16/88. Less than a week after transplant into compost, all 6 plants doing much better; first signs of budding:
- Tap-water marigolds: 1
- Crystal-water marigolds: 1 (smaller)

Water-Hardness Test: 7/16/88. Water in both bottles at least one week:
- Tap water: 7 gpg
- Crystal water: 6½ gpg

APPENDIX C

Preliminary Planning of Crystal-Power Survey

D_{ate:} 3/10/88

It's occurred to me that I should put my OB research techniques to work, trying to test my hypothesis that crystals act as a placebo/ mandala. Population, of course, would be crystal workers—believers and advocates. Possible samples include readers of *Fate, Horoscope,* and other pyschic magazines, plus customers at crystal shops, like Silbey Uma's and Dael Walker in Pacheco.

The questionnaire must be a bit subtle so as to not give away the hypothesis, and must appeal to believers so they will want to fill it out and send it in. One of the corollaries to my hypothsis is that the "crystal-energy recipient" must be aware that the crystal worker is trying to affect and/or heal him/her. Thus, if I ask questions about the *distance* at which crystals work, and whether or not the recipient must be present (i.e., know about), I will be indirectly learning if the crystals *can be* acting as placebos.

For the placebo effect to work, the patient must *think* he is getting the actual drug.

Date: 3/11/88

I've revised and pared down my questionnaire to fit on one page (see 9–3 above); I even changed the word *ceremony* to *energizing,* figuring that would appeal to crystal workers more.

I've also run a Statpac test of my 2nd alternative hypothesis:

H(A2): Those who note that crystals work best while the recipient is present are really noticing the placebo effect, and thus will find that so-called crystal energies do not work well at a distance, while those who believe they *can* affect recipients not present will also believe the crystal energies can extend to almost any distance.

Statistical Test of Hypothesis: Chi-square test of question 8 against questions 8a and 9 will find that Yes's and No's on 8 differ significantly on questions 8a and 9; otherwise reject hypothesis.

APPENDIX D

Complete Results of Crystal-Power Survey

Descriptive Statistics

Q1: How Interested?	Number	%
F = friends	51	26.8
O = other	60	31.6
PF = psychic fair	9	4.7
R = reading	59	31.1
SM = Shirley MacLaine	11	5.8
	---	---
Total	190	100.0

Missing cases = 0
Response % = 100.0

Q2: How Long?	No.	%
A = less than 1 year	21	11.1
B = 1 to 2 years	39	20.6
C = 2 to 5 years	40	21.2
D = more than 5 yrs	89	47.1
	---	---
Total	189	100.0

Missing cases = 1
Response % = 99.5

Q3: Sex

F = female	129	67.9
M = male	61	32.1
Total	190	100.0

Missing cases = 0
Response % = 100.0

Q4: Age

A = under 18	2	1.1
B = 18 to 25	9	4.8
C = 25 to 40	51	27.0
D = 40 to 60	92	48.7
E = over 60	35	18.5
Total	189	100.0

Missing cases = 1
Response % = 99.5

Q5: Own Crystals?

	No.	%
N = no	18	9.5
Y = yes	172	90.5
Total	190	100.0

Missing cases = 0
Response % = 100.0

Q5b: Value?

A = $0-$50	62	36.5
B = $50-$100	26	15.3
C = $100-$200	19	11.2
D = $200-$500	22	12.9
E = over $500	41	24.1
Total	170	100.0

Missing cases = 20
Response % = 89.5

Q6: Wear Crystals?

N = no	51	27.0
Y = yes	138	73.0
Total	189	100.0

Missing cases = 1
Response % = 99.5

Q6b: How Often?

	No.	**%**
A = once a month	25	18.2
B = once a week	20	14.6
C = daily	36	26.3
D = always	56	40.9
Total	137	100.0

Missing cases = 53
Response % = 72.1 %

Q7: Crystal Worker?

N = no	60	31.6
Y = yes	130	68.4
	——	——
Total	190	100.0

Missing cases = 0
Response % = 100.0

Multiresponse Analysis: Uses of Crystals

No. of cases = 190	**Count**	**%**
Q7b: Self-Healing	106	55.8
Q7c: Healing Others	73	38.4
Q7d: Healing at Distance	54	28.4
Q7e: Meditation/Self-Improvement	110	57.9
Q7f: Astral Projection	36	18.9
Q7g: ESP	65	34.2
Q7h: Channeling	37	19.5
Q7i: Influencing	41	21.6
Q7j: Other	47	24.7
Q8: Recipients Participate?	**No.**	**%**
N = no	49	35.5
Y = yes	89	64.5
	——	——
Total	138	100.0

Missing cases = 52
Response % = 72.6

Q8b: Nonparticipating Success

A = not at all	18	15.9
B = somewhat	57	50.4
C = very	38	33.6
Total	113	100.0

Missing cases = 77
Response % = 59.5

Q9: Maximum Distance

	No.	%
A = same room	26	18.8
B = 100 feet	1	0.7
C = 1 mile	5	3.6
D = 100 miles	2	1.4
E = no limit	80	58.0
F = other	24	17.4
Total	138	100.0

Missing cases 52
Response % = 72.6

Q10: Tell Recipient?

N = no	58	40.0
S = sometimes	66	45.5
Y = yes	21	14.5
Total	145	100.0

Missing cases = 45
Response % = 76.3

Q11: Willing to Test?

N = no	15	8.1
Y = yes	171	91.9
Total	186	100.0

Missing cases = 4
Response % = 97.9

Questionnaire Source	No.	%
F = *Fate*	178	93.7
LJ = *Lapidary Journal*	12	6.3
Total	190	100.0

Missing cases = 0
Response % 100.0

State	No.	%
AL =	1	0.5
AR =	2	1.1
AZ =	5	2.6
CA =	30	15.8
CAN =	1	0.5
CO =	5	2.6
CT =	4	2.1
DE =	2	1.1
FL =	9	4.7
GA =	5	2.6
ID =	2	1.1
IL =	8	4.2

Appendix D: Complete Results of Crystal-Power Survey

State	No.	%
IN =	5	2.6
KS =	1	0.5
KY =	4	2.1
MA =	5	2.6
MD =	1	0.5
MI =	10	5.3
MN =	4	2.1
MO =	8	4.2
MS =	1	0.5
MT =	1	0.5
NC =	2	1.1
NJ =	3	1.6
NM =	1	0.5
NY =	11	5.8
OH =	8	4.2
OK =	8	4.2
OR =	4	2.1
PA =	5	2.6
SC =	4	2.1
TN =	1	0.5
TX =	3	1.6
VA =	4	2.1
WA =	14	7.4
WI =	4	2.1
WV =	2	1.1
WY =	2	1.1
Total	190	100.0

Missing cases = 0
Response % = 100.0

StatPac Gold Statistical Analysis Package
Crosstabs and Chi Square

Q8: RECIPIENTS PARTICIPATE? (*Y* Axis)
——BY——
Q9: MAXIMUM DISTANCE (*X* Axis)

No. Row Col. Tot.	same room A	100' B	1 mi. C	100 mi. D	no limit E	Other F	Row Tot.
	8	1	1	1	26	8	
No	17.8	2.2	2.2	2.2	57.8	17.8	45
	32.0	100.0	20.0	100.0	35.6	38.1	35.7
	6.3	0.8	0.8	0.8	20.6	6.3	
	17	0	4	0	47	13	
Yes	21.0	0.0	4.9	0.0	58.0	16.0	51
	68.0	0.0	80.0	0.0	I	64.4	61.964.3
	13.5	0.0	3.2	0.0	37.3	10.3	
Col.	25	1	5	1	73	21	126
Tot.	19.8	0.8	4.0	0.8	57.9	16.7	100.0

Chi square	=	4.34	Valid cases	=	126
Degrees of freedom	=	5	Missing cases	=	64
Probability of chance	=	0.502	Response rate	=	66.3
Cramer's V	=	.186	Somer's D	=	-.043 (X Indep)
Contingency coeff.	=	.182	Somer's D	=	-.023 (Y Indep)
Tau-A	=	-.014	Somer's D	=	-.03 (Symm)
Tau-C	=	-.028	Gamma	=	-.051
Entropy	=	2.558	Lambda	=	.044
Distribution index	=	.713			

Q10: TELL RECIPIENT? (*Y* Axis)
——BY——
Q9: MAXIMUM DISTANCE (*X* Axis)

No. Row % Col. % Tot. %	same room A	100' B	1 mi. C	100 mi. D	no limit E	other F	Row tot. G
No	8	1	2	0	24	11	
	17.4	2.2	4.3	0.0	52.2	23.9	46
	33.3	100.0	50.0	0.0	30.8	50.0	35.1
	6.1	0.8	1.5	0.0	18.3	8.4	
Sometimes	4	0	1	2	47	10	
	6.3	0.0	1.6	3.1	73.4	15.6	64
	16.7	0.0	25.0	100.0	60.3	45.5	48.9
	3.1	0.0	0.8	1.5	35.9	7.6	
Yes	12	0	1	0	7	1	
	57.1	0.0	4.8	0.0	33.3	4.8	21
	50.0	0.0	25.0	0.0	9.0	4.5	16.0
	9.2	0.0	0.8	0.0	5.3	0.8	
Col.	24		4	2	78	22	131
Tot.	18.3	0.8	3.1	1.5	5 9.5	16.8	100.0

Chi square	=	35.416	Valid cases	=	131	
Degrees of freedom	=	10	Missing cases	=	59	
Probability of chance	=	0.000	Response rate	=	68.9	
Cramer's V	=	.368	Somer's D	=	-.288	(X Indep)
Contingency coeff.	=	.461	Somer's D	=	-.213	(Y Indep)
Tau-A	=	-.125	Somer's D	=	-.245	(Symm)
Tau-C	=	-.186	Gamma	=	-.321	
Entropy	=	2.903	Lambda	=	.164	
Distribution index	=	.696				

Spearman's Rank-Difference Correlation Analysis

Variables in the Analysis and No. of Valid Cases

Var.	Variable label	N
V2	*Q10: Tell Recipient?*	*145*
V1	*Q9: Maximum Distance*	*138*

Spearman's Rank-difference Correlation Matrix

			V2
V1	rs	I	0.3753
	p	I	0.0000

NOTES

Chapter 1

1. "New Age Harmonies," Otto Friedrich, *Time,* Dec. 7, 1987, pp. 62–72.

2. "Deformation Induced Structural Defects in Cerium," G. P. Mohanty and Lawrence Jerome, *Journal de Physique,* May 1979, C5–381–82.

3. *Astrology Disproved,* Lawrence Jerome, Prometheus Books, Buffalo, N.Y., 1977.

Chapter 2

1. *The Crystal Book,* Dael Walker, The Crystal Company, Sunol, Calif., 1983, p. 28.

2. *Focus on Crystals,* Edmund Harold, Ballantine Books, New York, 1986, p. 6.

3. *The Crystal Connection,* Randall N. and Vicki Baer, Harper & Row, San Francisco, 1986, p. xv.

4. *Focus on Crystals,* p. 19.

5. *Windows of Light,* Randall N. and Vicki Baer, Harper & Row, San Francisco, 1984, p. 6.

6. *Insight: Hinduism Today: A Four-Page Introduction to the Crystal Lingam, San Marga and Iraivan Temple,* Hindu Businessmen's Association of Northern California, Hanamaulu, Hawaii, Oct., 1987, p. 1.

7. *Focus on Crystals,* p. 66.

8. "Jewels of Enlightenment," Marguerite Elsbeth Chandler, *Horoscope,* Dec., 1987, pp. 19–21, 114.

9. *Windows of Light,* p. xiv.

10. *The Crystal Book,* pp. 16-17.

Chapter 3

1. *Minerals and Man,* Cornelius Huribut, Random House, New York, 1968, p. 228.

2. *Shamanism: Archaic Techniques of Ecstasy,* Mircea Eliade, Princeton University Press, Princeton, N.J., 1964, p. 4.

3. *Pomo Shaman* (a film), University of California Extension Media Center, Berkeley, Calif., 1964.

4. "Quartz: Gem of Legend," Ron Bodoh, *Fate,* May 1986, p. 79.

5. *The Magic of Precious Stones,* Mellie Uyldert, Turnstone Press, Wellingborough, England, 1981, p. 53.

6. *The Curious Lore of Precious Stones,* George Kunz, Dover Books, New York, 1971, pp. 31, 343.

7. *Astrology Disproved,* p. 70–71.

8. *Curious Lore of Precious Stones,* pp. 176–77.

9. Citied in *Crystal Gazing,* N. W. Thomas, London, 1905, pp. xxiv, xxx.

10. *Curious Lore of Precious Stones,* p. 180.

11. *Shamans, Mystics and Doctors,* Sudhir Kakar, Alfred A. Knopf, New York, 1982, p. 32.

12. *The Crystal Book,* pp. 35–36.

Chapter 5

1. *Mineralogy for Students,* 2nd ed., M. H. Battey, Longman, London, 1981, p. 159.

2. *Electronics Six,* ed., Harry Mileaf, Hayden Book Co., Rochelle Park, N.J., 1976, p. 6–29.

3. *Laser: Supertool of the 1980s,* Jeff Hecht and Dick Teresi, Ticknor & Fields, New York, 1982, p. 23.

Chapter 6

1. "Crystal Mania: Romanticizing the Stone," Don Oldenburg, *Washington Post,* Nov. 13, 1987, p. D5.

2. *Basic Statistical Analysis,* Richard C. Sprinthall, Addison-Wesley Publishing Co., Reading, Mass., 1983, pp. 223–24.

3. "Placebo Effects in Medicine, Psychotherapy, and Psychoanalysis," A. K. Shapiro, *Handbook of Pyschotherapy and Behavior Change,* Wiley, New York, 1971.

4. "Of the Force of Imagination," Michel de Montaigne, Great Books of the Western World, Vol. 25, Encyclopaedia Britannica, Chicago, 1952, p. 40.

5. "The Placebo Effect Reconsidered," by Alfred O. Berg, *Journal of Family Practice* 17, no. 4 (1983), p. 647.

6. *The Writings of Thomas Jefferson,* Vol. 9, P. L. Ford, Putnam, New York, 1898, p. 78.

7. "Placebo Effects in Medicine, Psychotherapy, and Psychoanalysis."

8. "The Powerful Placebo," Henry K. Beecher, *Journal of the American Medical Association* 159, 1955, pp. 1602–1606.

9. "The Placebo Effect: A Neglected Asset in the Care of Patients," Herbert Benson and Mark D. Epstein, *Journal of the American Medical Association* 232, no. 12, (1975), p. 1225.

10. *Free Yourself from Pain,* David E. Bresler, Simon and Schuster, New York, 1979, p. 146.

11. "The Placebo Effect," p. 1226.

12. "Physician and Patient Attitudes as Factors Influencing the Placebo Response in Depression," Gilbert Honigfeld, *Diseases of the Nervous System,* June, 1963, pp. 343–47.

13. "Suggestibility and Placebo Effect," Joseph A. Deltito, *Clinical and Experimental Rheumatology* 3, 1985, p. 97.

14. "The Powerful Placebo," p. 1603.

15. "The Placebo Response in Pain Control," Frederick J. Evans, *Psychopharmacology Bulletin* 17, April, 1981, p. 73.

16. "The Placebo Effect," p. 1226.

17. *Shamans, Mystics and Doctors,* p. 39.

18. "Credibility of Placebo Transcutaneious Nerve Stimulation and Acupuncture," J. Petrie and B. Hazlemen, *Clinical and Experimental Rheumatology* 3, 1985, p. 151.

Chapter 7

1. Paraphrased from a radio broadcast, KGO Radio, San Francisco, Oct. 18, 1988.

2. *New Mind, New Body: Biofeedback: New Directions for the Mind,* Barbara B. Brown, Harper & Row, New York, 1974, p. 139.

3. "The Placebo Response in Pain Control," p. 74.

4. *The Living Brain,* Walter W. Grey, 1963, pp. 85–123.

5. *The Power of Alpha-Thinking—Miracle of the Mind,* Jess Stearn, Signet Books, New York, 1976.

Chapter 8

1. Table 8–1 was adapted from *Birth and Planetary Data Gathered Since 1949,* Michel and Françoise Gauquelin, Laboratoire D'Etude des Relations Entre Rythmes Cosmiques et Psychophysiologiques, Series C, Vol. 1, p. 54.

2. Cited in *Real Magic,* Philip Bonewits, Coward, McCann & Geoghegan, New York, 1970, pp. 63–67.

3. *Biological Order,* Andre Lwoff, MIT Press, Cambridge, 1962, pp. 95–96.

Chapter 9

1. *The Crystal Connection,* p. xv.
2. *Astrology Disproved,* p. 136.
3. Personal conversation with Dael Walker, Mar. 31, 1988.
4. Ibid.
5. *Ecology and Field Biology,* Robert L. Smith, Harper & Row, New York, 1966, p. 598.
6. "The *Fate* Crystal Survey," *Fate,* Aug. 1988, p. 73.
7. "The Crystal Contingent," Merle Berk, *Lapidary Journal,* June 1988, p. 68.

Chapter 10

1. *The Psychic Source Book: How to Choose and Use a Psychic,* quoted in "Crystal Gazing in the New Age of Psychic Power," Elise T. Chisolm, *San Jose Mercury News,* Oct. 19, 1988, p. 10C.

INDEX